Walter Waddington Shirley

Some Account of the Church in the Apostolic Age

To which is Added an Essay on Dogmatic Preaching

Walter Waddington Shirley

Some Account of the Church in the Apostolic Age
To which is Added an Essay on Dogmatic Preaching

ISBN/EAN: 9783337162559

Printed in Europe, USA, Canada, Australia, Japan

Cover: Foto ©Lupo / pixelio.de

More available books at **www.hansebooks.com**

SOME ACCOUNT OF
THE CHURCH
IN THE APOSTOLIC AGE:

TO WHICH IS ADDED,

AN ESSAY
ON DOGMATIC PREACHING.

BY THE LATE
WALTER WADDINGTON SHIRLEY, D.D.
REGIUS PROFESSOR OF ECCLESIASTICAL HISTORY
AND CANON OF CHRIST CHURCH.

SECOND EDITION.

Oxford:
AT THE CLARENDON PRESS.
M DCCC LXXIV.

CONTENTS.

	PAGE
SOME ACCOUNT OF THE CHURCH IN THE APOSTOLIC AGE	1
AN ESSAY ON DOGMATIC PREACHING .	141

PREFACE.

THE following chapters on the Apostolic Age are all that the lamented Author lived to write of a projected manual of ancient Church History. But, fragmentary as they are, it is thought that they possess sufficient unity and completeness, as a sketch of the leading features of the period with which they deal, to warrant their publication.

They had not been finally revised by Dr. Shirley when he was taken from us, in the midst of hopeful and fruitful labours, on the 20th of November, 1866. The Editor is responsible for some verbal corrections, for nearly all the headings of the chapters, and for the references enclosed within brackets.

The essay or paper on Dogmatic Preaching, written for the Church Congress of 1866, and read on that occasion by a friend in the Author's absence through illness, has been included in the volume.

W. BRIGHT.

UNIVERSITY COLLEGE, OXFORD,
March 5, 1867.

SOME ACCOUNT

OF

THE APOSTOLIC AGE.

B

SOME ACCOUNT OF THE APOSTOLIC AGE.

CHAPTER I.

From the Day of Pentecost to the Martyrdom of St. Stephen.

THE day of Pentecost is the true era of the Church of Christ, for on it was bestowed that gift of an indwelling Spirit which is her distinctive inheritance. On it was completed that initial work upon which she is divinely founded. For the gift of the Holy Spirit is in fact the complement of the Incarnation. It was the beginning of Christ's work that the Godhead should be clothed with humanity; it was the end of it that humanity should be exalted by the presence of an indwelling Godhead.

As the festival of thanksgiving for the first-fruits of the yearly harvest, perhaps as the anniversary of the giving of the Law from Sinai, the day of Pentecost was already sacred to the heart of every Israelite. It was to be hallowed henceforward by a new and deeper consecration, as the day of the firstfruits of the Christian Church, and of the promulgation of that new law, of which the code of Sinai was the pale and distant shadow.

On that day, as by a common impulse, the whole body of the disciples was gathered under a single roof; and that great gift, for which they had been taught to wait, was then suddenly bestowed. The Holy Ghost descended upon them in a form peculiarly expressive of the power which His indwelling presence would bestow. The sound from heaven as of a mighty tempest borne impetuously along; the cloven tongue of fire resting harmless upon the head of each individual disciple; and not least, the gift of languages,—were eloquent of the Divine Spirit, so impetuous in His entrance, so gently fervent in His indwelling power: eloquent too at once of the strife and storm which was to mark the outer life of the Church, and of the depth of her inward peace—of the unending variety of the message which she was to utter to every heart and to every kindred of mankind, and of the secret bond which, amidst all outward difference, was to unite for evermore the souls of all her believing children.

The impression produced on the multitude must have amazed those who thought of the slender measure of apparent success which had attended the ministry of the Lord. It was to be in divine things as in human; the disciples were to reap the harvest sown by the Master. When St. Peter spoke, on behalf of the twelve apostles, of the name of Jesus as the power through which the miracles of the Spirit had been given, there were added at once to the disciples no less than three thousand souls. Thus then the Church of Christ was founded. And as it was to be a spiritual society, destined to walk not by sight but by faith, so from its very foundation it possessed this striking peculiarity—that only a small proportion of its members had been the personal disciples of the Lord. No reasonable estimate of the first disciples will carry their number beyond six or seven hundred. Yet to this original body were added, on the very day when the disciples became a Church, no less than three thousand souls. And so it was that from the very first the thought of Christ in His Church must have been far less of the Teacher Jesus than of the Ascended Lord, who had dispensed to His disciples the gifts of the Holy Spirit, who was the spring of their inner life, the centre of their adoring homage. It was, in a word, an unseen Christ who was worshipped in the Church from the beginning.

The first converts were beyond a doubt taken, almost without exception, from the lower orders of society. We are indeed told expressly that, even after a very sensible lapse of time, none but the people ventured to join the ranks of the disciples[a]; and it would seem that the conversion of Barnabas—a Levite, a Cypriot, and a man of landed property—was in more ways than one an event of importance in the history of the infant society. It was a first indication that the Church might be expected to draw some of her converts not only from the wealthier classes, but from among the priests, of whom we learn afterwards that a great company was obedient to the faith[b], and, what was in the events more important than

[a] [Acts v. 13.]   [b] [Acts vi. 7.]

all, from the ranks of those Hellenistic Jews who were soon to give to the Church a St. Stephen and a St. Philip, and who in God's own time were to be the connecting link between a Jewish and a Gentile Christendom.

At first the disciples lived together, with a community, not indeed of property, but of the daily use of all worldly possessions, so complete as to become impossible when the Christian society diffused itself far beyond its original limits, or even when it passed from its first attitude of rapt and wondering adoration to struggle with the hard realities of life. Yet we can trace in this matter no abrupt change of habit, no startling decline from the fervour of a first love. On the contrary, the life of the very first Christians was little more than an application to very simple exceptional circumstances of that largeness of heart and hand which, long after Apostolic days, provided a constant maintenance for the sick, the widows, and the aged, who bore the name of Christ. If for a time they had all things in common in a more absolute sense than came afterwards to be the case, it was because they were given up for a short while to a life which was little else than a continual act of worship. They observed with a quickened devotion the daily hours of prayer which at morning, noon, and night drew worshippers to the courts of the Temple; they superadded the solemn breaking of bread from house to house— the daily Eucharist, which was the peculiar privilege and glory of their Christian name.

And while the sacrament which the first disciples thus celebrated day by day[c] was to them, in the great secret of its power, what it has been to the Church till now, it had in some minor but not unimportant respects a peculiar significance to them.

It was to them, as it is to us, the visible expression of the presence of our ascended Lord. But how incalculable the difference in the meaning of that presence to them! He had left them but a few days or weeks; He had but now returned in the person of the promised Comforter: and they were now permitted to partake of the broken bread, as the emblem of His restoration to them[d]. It was

[c] [Acts ii. 46.]
[d] A comparison of Acts i. 14 and ii. 46 seems to suggest, what in itself we should expect, that before the day of Pentecost the Eucharist was not administered.

to them, as it is to us, the pledge of our Lord's return. But to them it was accompanied with an exulting belief that their own eyes should see the world bow down before the Crucified, and witness His speedy return to be the Judge of quick and dead. Their expectation of the future of the Church had yet to be chastened, to be spiritualized, to be enlarged. They had still to pass through a process of patient discipline, like that which under the earthly ministry of our Lord had subdued and elevated the yet grosser notions of the original twelve apostles.

The Eucharist was again to them, as it is to us, the one great act of Christian sacrificial worship; in its outward form the simplest of all acts of sacrifice, in its inner meaning the highest and most difficult of all, as expressing the self-renouncing love by which the Christian becomes one with Christ. But to the first disciples, accustomed to a ritual in which the sacrifice of animals was the very central act of worship, the institution of a new and spiritual sacrifice must have had a significance which it is hard for us to realize. From the very first it must have produced a secret loosening of the heart from that part of the Temple service on which their fellow Jews still centred their highest adoration. They attended the service of the Temple; but it was the Temple as the house, not of sacrifice, but of prayer. And to the depth of the feeling which here finds its expression the history of the Church offers a striking testimony. Gathered out of every religion under heaven, and imbibing from without the germs of a hundred heresies, the Church has never yet been troubled by an attempt to erect within its pale a system of sacrifices such as most of its converts had been taught from childhood to regard as an essential of worship. The Eucharist has had power absolutely to efface the craving.

Two more points complete the picture which we have received of the earliest Church of Christ. "They continued in the doctrine of the apostles and the fellowship." The doctrine of the apostles, one and indivisible, was an essential bond of union. And it may have been among the reasons why Christ willed that for twelve long years[e] His apostles should

---

[e] The well-known tradition [see Euseb. v. 18] that our Lord commanded the apostles to remain for twelve years at Jeru-

confine their action to the immediate neighbourhood of Jerusalem, that by this means alone the necessary deference to apostolic authority could be so impressed upon the Church as to retain a lasting hold when the Christian name was diffused far beyond the possible limits of their collective supervision and control.

And because the doctrine was one, therefore the fellowship was one also: for the fellowship was the expression of the doctrine. The Church was before all things a brotherhood; Christianity was emphatically "that way" or mode of life. But it was a life which derived its peculiar character from the fact that it was impregnated with a belief in the life and death of Christ, with the sense of His spiritual presence, and the hope of His personal return. It had that in common with fanaticism that it removed men from the current of common motives, and led them to make light of the things which attract and govern mankind; it had that also

---

salem, must have been current in the middle of the second century. The contrast between its perfect definiteness and the reserve of our Lord's words on the subject of times and seasons as recorded in the New Testament cannot fail to strike us. But the tradition tallies with the fact, to which probably it owes its precision if not its origin.

of which fanaticism has been the sure and deadly enemy—deep and ardent love of man to his fellow man. Never on this earth had man been so much to his brother man as he now became in a society founded upon a belief which could not but depreciate the value of every earthly object. It had that in common with the asceticism of the Essenian and Therapeutic communities, that it bound men together in the tie of a common life, and by the strength of a religious principle; it had that in absolute contrast with every form of Jewish asceticism, that instead of withdrawing itself in stern and silent self-discipline from the polluting contact of society, it went out to the conquest of the world, radiant with overflowing joy and exulting in the consciousness of power.

The unruffled peace which marked the first days of the Church was broken by the consequences of a miracle wrought by St. Peter and St. John. The healing of the lame man who sat begging at the Beautiful Gate of the Temple was far from being the first which had been worked by the hands of the apostles. But this was worked at the most public gate of the Temple, at the crowded hour of prayer; and the whole congregation could see the beggar, whose familiar face they knew, walking into the Temple and praising God for his recovery. The crowd ran together, forgetting the service of the Temple, to hear from the lips of St. Peter that the resurrection of the crucified Jesus was the cause of this miracle of healing.

The enmity of three distinct classes of men was by this act directed towards the Church. The Captain of the Temple came upon the apostles, indignant at the breach of order and the scene of confusion which disturbed the sacred services. The priests had, besides, their own ground of resentment in the unauthorized teaching of religion; the Sadducees, in the turn which that teaching took, and the doctrine of the resurrection of the dead. The two apostles were arrested and brought before the Sanhedrin; but the popular enthusiasm, roused by the great miracle, proved the protection of the prisoners, and they were dismissed with a command to abstain for the future from their teaching.

The return of the apostles to the Church was greeted with something more than thankfulness. It was the occasion of the earliest hymn of Christian praise of which the substance has been preserved to us. And that hymn speaks not only of gratitude for the past, but of a renewed sense of the fact that the efforts of Herod and of Pilate, of Roman procurator and of Jewish Sanhedrin, were controlled by a higher power. It read in the persecution, not a motive for reserve, but a call for fresh courage and increased boldness of speech.

The period which followed this first persecution is marked, in fact, by a visible increase of courage. Unabashed by the rebuke of the Sanhedrin, the apostles keep the very scene of the arrest as a kind of head-quarters for the Church. "They were all," we are told, "with one accord in Solomon's porch." The unity of the believers is unbroken; it is, if possible, closer than ever. Miracles are multiplied; the preaching of the apostles is full of power; "the Son of Consolation" joins the ranks of the disciples. The two half-believers who had dared to question the searching presence of the Spirit fall dead by an awful judgment. The streets of Jerusalem become crowded with the beds and couches of the sick, who expect life and healing from the very shadow of St. Peter as he passes. The fame of the Church begins to be spread even beyond the city; and the inhabitants of the neighbouring villages come flocking in, and bring their sick to be healed [f].

It no longer needs a disturbance of the Temple worship to bring down upon the Church fresh acts of persecution. The whole sect of the Sadducees, with the high priest at their head, takes the lead in the movement, and commits the apostles to the common prison.

But the position of the persecutors was one full of difficulty. The people favoured the apostles; and the favour of that turbulent populace counted for much in Jerusalem; and the Pharisees were lukewarm enemies of a sect whose chief crime might appear to be that they taught the resurrection of the dead. The miraculous deliverance of the apostles from their prison completed the embarrassment of the Sanhedrin; the extreme party was overawed, and the milder counsels of the Pharisee Gamaliel were accepted. The apostles were scourged and dismissed.

But there was that already in preparation which was before long to give birth to a

[f] Acts iv. 36; v. 12, 15, 16.

persecution of a very different character. The disciples of our Lord Himself were in all probability drawn wholly, or all but wholly, from the ranks of the Hebrew Jews. The Hebrews, as they loved to call themselves, looked down with a pride of a severer nationality and a more strict observance upon those of their countrymen who had adopted the language and the manners of the Greek. The Hellenist, on the other hand, with a wider circle of ideas and a larger appreciation of the civilization which adorned the Gentile world, returned the cold pride of the Hebrew with the charge of narrow-mindedness and bigotry. The two great sections of the Jewish nation thus held aloof from each other, divided by a line as sharp, probably, as that which parted the Pharisee from the Herodian or the Sadducee. And, in fact, no doubt the lines of sectarian division corresponded roughly to that which parted the Hebrew from the Hellenist. The religious sympathies of the Hebrew were, as a rule, with the Pharisees; the laxer nationality corresponded, very generally, to the laxer creed. The first intimation which we receive of the presence of both these elements within the pale of the Church is given to us by their discord. As the number of the disciples multiplied, and as room was thereby given at once for difference and mismanagement, there arose a complaint from the Hellenists that their widows were neglected in the daily distribution of alms. The answer of the apostles to the complaint was the memorable appointment of the Seven, with the primary duty of administering the charities of the Church. There can be no question, from a mere survey of the names [g], that the Hellenists were largely represented; and the most distinguished of the whole body, St. Stephen, was beyond doubt a Hellenist. He, and at least one other, united, like the deacons of later days [h], certain spiritual functions with the humbler duties of his office. Stephen became, in fact, one of the foremost preachers of the whole infant Church. He preached especially to Hellenists; and his preaching was deeply coloured by his Hellenistic training. Less rivetted than his Hebrew brethren by the overpowering force of association to the Holy

[g] A Greek name would not absolutely prove the possessor to have been a Hellenist.

[h] The question whether the Seven were deacons in the strict sense of the word I reserve for future consideration.

City, and even to the very Temple itself, he saw with a clearness which as yet had been given to no Christian preacher, how little the course of God's dealings, even under the older covenant, had confined His favour to a single chosen locality; how little, too, it had corresponded, at any one time, to the popular belief and the popular expectation of the Jews. He could read, in the past career and present conduct of his countrymen, a sure augury that a mighty change was at hand in the religious condition of the nation and of the world. He could bear with steady and undimmed eye the thought of a future in which Jerusalem should be no longer the religious capital of the world, nor the Temple the one centre of the worship of the true God. It is the depth of historical perspective which is so remarkable in the preaching of St. Stephen. St. Peter assuredly believed with as firm a faith the declaration of his Lord that the day would come when not one stone of the Temple should stand upon another. He intimates, if less boldly yet with sufficient clearness, his fear that the Jews, as a nation, would reject their own Messiah. And he warns them, in no doubtful terms, that He whom they rejected would return to be their Judge. But between the rejection and the judgment there is, as it were, a vacuum. There is nothing in the earlier teaching of St. Peter or of St. John, as given to us in the Acts of the Apostles, which suggests the thought of a new career for the Church, intermediate between the final rejection of Christ by the Jewish nation and His return to be the Judge of quick and dead. On that portion of the future the eye of the twelve had not yet been fixed. It was given to St. Stephen to catch the first glimpse of that new land of promise which was viewed for the Church upon earth. The Jews might reject the Messiah, and Jerusalem might become a heap of ruins; the Church, he foresaw, would survive her rejection by the chosen people, and the ruin of the very Temple itself.

There were doubtless chords of sympathy which such a teaching would touch in the hearts of some who, like St. Stephen himself, combined the more cosmopolitan tone of a Hellenistic training with an earnest and religious life. But to the mass of the Jews, to the mass even of the Hellenists, it was the bitterest word which had yet been uttered in the name of Jesus Christ.

A sect of devout Jews, living a saintly life, and diffusing around them acts of healing and beneficence, might be an object of jealousy to the priests, of theological hostility to the Sadducee; it could hardly be other than acceptable to the general mass of the people. And such, until now, had been the infant Church. Even after the second summons of the apostles before the Sanhedrin, they boldly maintained their head-quarters within the very Temple itself, in the public porch of Solomon: multitudes were daily added to the disciples; and however coldly they might be looked upon in higher quarters, the people still "magnified them." But from the day when St. Stephen became prominent among Christian teachers the whole scene is changed. On the one hand, the Church begins to make her way among a class which as yet she had touched but little, and "a great company of the priests became obedient to the faith." On the other, the national feeling was aroused. The quick ear of the people caught the note of a teaching which seemed to suggest that the Temple should not be eternal; and for the first time they combined with the scribes and elders to institute a persecution against the Church of Christ.

Nor was the hostility of the people the only element in the persecution which was aroused by the preaching of St. Stephen. The Pharisees, who on the first arrest of the apostles had been altogether silent, who on the second had been, through Gamaliel, the advocates of the milder course, were now the front and head of the opposition. The mature and temperate Gamaliel has given up the lead to the impassioned energy of his disciple; and populace, Sadducee, and zealot are led on against the common enemy by the strong will and the ardent genius of the young Saul of Tarsus.

CHAPTER II.

From the Martyrdom of St. Stephen to the Council of Jerusalem.

AT the time of the martyrdom of St. Stephen from eight to ten years had elapsed since the foundation of the Church. She must have included within her pale Galilean disciples even from the first. We learn incidentally that she had members even at Damascus. But we hear almost nothing of her activity beyond the limits of Jerusalem and the neighbouring villages. She had gained in numbers and in strength, and in a clearer sense of her mission; —her diffusion was yet to come. We pass with the Sauline persecution into a new stage of her history. Almost all the disciples, numbering many thousands, were now dispersed from Jerusalem. They took refuge in the more remote parts of Judæa, in Samaria, in Cyprus, in Phœnicia; and wherever they went, they of course diffused the Gospel. We follow them to four points in particular.

1. While one of the Seven was the first to suggest to the Church the thought of a wider and less local career, another was the first to break the charmed circle which had until now confined the Church to the race or the faith of Abraham. Philip the Evangelist took refuge in Samaria. He there preached to a people who were regarded by the Jews with a feeling of contemptuous aversion, as an ignoble copy of themselves. Aliens in race, strangers to the strongest nationality by which men have ever been united, they had adopted the rite of circumcision, and a pale and mutilated imitation of the ritual and the religion of Moses. Philip, with the recollection of his Lord before him, threw away his prejudices, and met them on the ground of their common hope of a Messiah. But the way had been prepared for his work, not only by the visit of our Lord Himself to Sychem, but by the presence of very different influences.

Nothing is more painful in the history of the earlier Empire of Rome than the deep despair of truth which had settled heavily upon the whole classical world. The Epicurean and the

Stoic philosophies divided the allegiance if not the affections of men, and based their opposite views of life upon a common despair of any truth which was not attested by the senses. The irrepressible craving of man for intercourse with the unseen world, degraded by the prevailing materialism, took refuge in occult arts; the practice of magic grew apace; the magician rose to the dignity of a religious teacher, and increased his importance by adding to the marvels of his art a kind of theosophic teaching, for which he generally found a basis in the religious systems of the East, which still preserved some share of vitality, and which possessed in the highest degree the dreamy indistinctness for which materialism has often so strange an affinity. Of these men perhaps the most celebrated at this particular time was one Simon of Gittum, better known to us by the name of Simon Magus. The nature of his doctrine we shall have occasion to consider more exactly hereafter. Here it may suffice to say that the basis of his system was Zoroastrian, and that he gave out himself to be a great Æon or spirit, derived by emanation from the Eternal Fire who was the Supreme Diety. His presence in Samaria, where he had long established himself, accustomed the people to look for miracles as the natural attestation of a new system of doctrine, and in this way prepared them to receive with peculiar readiness the teaching of the Evangelist St. Philip, who made many converts. Simon was himself convinced of the reality of the power possessed by the new teacher; he wondered at his miracles; he confessed himself surpassed, and submitted to the rite of baptism. But his astonishment was not yet at its height. Philip was only an Evangelist, and had not therefore the apostolic power of imparting the Holy Spirit by the laying on of hands. Lost in amazement at the visible results of this act, and profoundly disbelieving all the while the existence of anything divine, Simon desired to buy of the apostles the possession of their wonderful secret. The stern rebuke of St. Peter alarmed for a moment even his hardened heart. But it was but for a moment. Simon, ever versatile, retired awhile from Samaria. He engrafted into his system such elements of Christianity as admitted of easy adaptation, and became, as the first Gnostic, the founder of a class of heresies which were destined to exercise an almost incalculable influence on the fortunes of early Christendom. We shall meet with him again. It is for the first contact of the Church with the spirit of Gnosticism, hardly less than for the first approach towards a conversion of Gentiles to Christianity, that the visit of St. Philip to Samaria is an epoch in the history of the early Church.

2. To the same great Evangelist it was given to loosen in another direction the hold of Jewish exclusiveness upon the Church of Christ. The conversion of Samaria was followed by that of the Ethiopian eunuch. The outward rite of circumcision, which bridged over the gulf between the Jews and the half-believing Samaritans, was exactly the one which was wanting to the chamberlain of Queen Candace. He had come to the Temple to worship; he was a Jew in faith and heart; he was only debarred from becoming a full member of the religious commonwealth of Israel by the ceremonial precept which forbade him the right of circumcision. His was indeed a case for which the later prophets had expressed so large a tenderness that the outward defect was probably but

little considered even among the stricter Jews. It is not the less true, and it is most strikingly suggested by the order of St. Luke's narrative, that to combine the ceremonial shortcoming of the eunuch with the imperfect faith of the Samaritan, is to arrive at the admission of Gentiles.

3. Among the places which were visited by the dispersed disciples, by far the most important in itself, and for the history of the Church, was the city of Antioch on the Orontes, the third in rank and population of the whole Empire of Rome. The disciples who took refuge there were natives of Cyprus and Cyrene: they were therefore Hellenists. Their friends and converts at Antioch were men of the same language, and thus, by their means, a Church was planted, and planted for the first time, upon a Hellenistic basis. Of all the earlier communities the original language was Hebrew. Of the Church at Antioch the original language was Greek [a]. And in this fact,

[a] The popular notion derived from the subsequent history of the Church of Antioch, that the first converts there were Gentiles, has biassed even critics like Meyer, Tischendorf, and Alford, to read Ἕλληνας for Ἑλληνιστὰς in Acts xi. 20, confessedly against the weight of MS. and patristic authority. As

was implied that profound difference of tone which fitted it to become at no distant time the mother of Gentile Christendom.

4. While these various events were preparing the way for the coming admission of Gentiles within the pale of the Church, Christ was preparing His own instrument for the work. The flight of the persecuted drew after them the fury of the arch-persecutor. As he was nearing Damascus, he was struck to the ground by the brightness of a heavenly vision, and Saul of Tarsus rose from the earth a convert. His conversion brought to the service of the faith the one man who was fitted for the work of blending Jew and Gentile in one undivided Church. His wonderful career is due, under

we shall see hereafter, the reading Ἕλληνας does as much violence to history as it does to textual criticism. I may remark [the Author intended to cancel this passage, and to revert to the point afterwards], by the way, that it is a mistake to suppose that the sense of the passage requires a contrast between the Ἰουδαίοις of ver. 19 and the persons mentioned in ver. 20—an idea which has, it would seem, led to the insertion of καὶ after ἐλάλουν in ver. 20 in a small number of good MSS. The great importance of the Church of Antioch leads St. Luke to define more exactly the class of Jews among whom it was founded. Instances of this careful definition of the constituent elements of an important Church are frequent in the Acts of the Apostles. [Acts xiii. 43, 48; xiv.1; xvii. 4, 12.]

God, not only to the high spiritual gifts and to the warmth and tenderness of character which have ever centred on him so large a share of the reverent affection of Christians, but also to the unerring penetration with which he traced the bearing of great principles through the tangled maze of circumstances, and hardly less to antecedents which had trained him to appreciate alike the larger cultivation of the Greek and the severe uncompromising spirit of the Hebrew and the Pharisee.

Born at Tarsus, the capital of a Grecianized province, the seat of a Greek university, he received his early education in the presence of classical influences, to which the very style of his Epistles offers abundant evidence. But his father was a Hebrew. Hebrew was the language of his home. In Hebrew, and at Jerusalem, the home of every Hebrew influence, he completed his education at the feet of Gamaliel, the foremost doctor of the day. If there was a moment in the history of the Church when it seemed as if the door of faith would be opened to the Gentiles by the hands of men of the stamp of St. Stephen and St. Philip—Hellenists in language, Hellenists in every sympathy—it is easy to recognise, in many circumstances of the later life of St. Paul, of what value it was to him to have been not only a Hellenist by the training of his earlier years, but even yet more a Hebrew, by the deeper and more enduring ties of home and of later education.

With his conversion the persecution of which he was the life seems to have died away. It must in any case have ceased with the appointment of Agrippa to the government of Judæa and Samaria (A. D. 41), for that appointment put an end to the anarchy during which alone the Sanhedrin could have granted the extraordinary commission which they placed in the hands of Saul.

The time of rest which followed was a time of quiet growth, marked only by one very memorable event.

The conversion of Cornelius is indeed the greatest epoch in the early history of the Church. If it was permitted to St. Stephen and St. Philip, or even to the nameless founders of the Hellenistic Church of Antioch, to prepare the way for the admission of Gentiles into the Church, that critical step was itself to be committed to no one less than to the very Chief of the Apostolic

College, and it was to be marked by circumstances which could leave no doubt either of the guidance of the Holy Spirit or of the momentous nature of the act. The word of an angel bade the centurion Cornelius send for the apostle Peter: to St. Peter a special vision announced that God had henceforth removed the barrier which parted the clean from the unclean; he was expressly commanded to go with the messengers, assured that God had sent them; and lastly, as Cornelius and his friends listened to the apostle's preaching, the Holy Spirit descended, as on the day of Pentecost, and on that day alone, without the intervention of any human hand. Thus was the adhesion of these Gentile converts marked out as almost a second foundation of the Church.

It may seem at first sight to be almost unaccountable that so clear an intimation of the will of God should not have been followed at once by a general diffusion of the Gospel among the Gentiles, and that a supernatural power once called out should not have immediately arrived at the result which its action was designed to accomplish. It is, however, in more true accordance with the economy of miraculous power, as discovered to us throughout the Bible, when we see that, as in secular history, the enunciation of a great principle, even when propounded with a more than human sanction, is not followed at once by the consequences which, sooner or later, flow inevitably from it.

In fact, even after the express direction of the Spirit in the crucial case of Cornelius, there remained to the conversion of the Gentiles obstacles of a magnitude which we may easily be tempted to forget.

Any Christian preacher, in fact, who should attempt to convey the Gospel message to the heathen, must have been prepared to state clearly in what relation his converts were to stand henceforward to the law of Moses. And to that momentous question there were three answers possible.

1. That they should be circumcised, and keep the Mosaic law. The two may be placed together, for it was everywhere admitted—at least in theory—that circumcision implied the keeping of the Law.

2. That they might become to the Christian Church what the proselyte of the gate was to the Jewish.

3. That they should be held entirely free from the Law.

Between the first and the last of these courses it was indeed possible that compromise might discover some intermediate position. There were none but these three which could be rested upon anything like a principle. And yet in the way of all of them there lay difficulties of principle, of practice, or of both, which if carefully weighed will suffice amply to explain how it was that the conversion of Cornelius did not lead more rapidly to the opening of the Church to the heathen.

1. With regard to the first course, of compelling circumcision and the observance of the Mosaic law, it may be observed :—

(*a.*) That it required of every convert to pass through the double process of conversion to Judaism itself, and also to something further which was erected as a superstructure upon it. Now when it is remembered that proselytes to Judaism were always few in number, and, as we know from the words of our Lord Himself[b], in no way distinguished for the elevation of their moral tone—despised by the heathen, and not

---

[b] [Matt. xxiii. 15.]

respected by the Jew—it is easy to perceive that to require men, as a condition of the acceptance of Christianity, to pass through initiation into such a body as this, was to place a barrier in the way of the conversion of the Gentile world which might well seem insuperable. To those at least who were convinced of the necessity of circumcision it must also have appeared that the Jewish nation was the natural channel of God's grace, and the conversion of the Jews the true field for their labours, and the only hope of the eventual conversion of the world. And in this reasonable belief they might easily be confirmed, not only by the older Covenant, which marked out the chosen people as the keepers of the Divine truth, but also by many words of the prophets, which seemed expressly to promise to the chosen people the adhesion of a converted world[c].

The natural effect, therefore, of a belief in the necessity of circumcision would be at once to withdraw the preacher from the field of heathen missions, and to throw obstacles of no common kind in the way of those casual converts to whom a knowledge of Christianity might still chance to come.

[c] [e. g. Isaiah xlix. 18 seq.; lx. 4 seq.; Zech. viii. 22, 23.]

(*b.*) But further: although the Hebrew Christians continued to observe the Law, their adoption of Christianity must powerfully have affected the strength of their allegiance to it. The displacement of the Temple sacrifice from its pre-eminence as the highest act of worship; the misgiving which this must have implied as to its further efficacy or meaning, and the haze of difficulty and confusion which must thus have been thrown upon many of the Jewish ordinances,—must needs have paralysed all missionary effort in which those questions were involved. A perplexed man may hold fast his own belief: he will never impart it to another.

(*c.*) And last, but not least, the indications given by the Holy Spirit to the Church were enough to throw serious doubt upon this course of action. The vision of St. Peter, thrice repeated, seemed emphatically to point to some large relaxation of those barriers which as yet had severed Jew and Gentile. The full gift of the Holy Ghost bestowed on men uncircumcised, and the absence of any command or even suggestion that circumcision should follow, all seemed to point to some freer course of action, and therefore to increase the perplexity of those who believed notwithstanding in the necessity of circumcision.

2. But if the objections to requiring the circumcision of heathen converts were so weighty, even for those who did not see with St. Paul all that the Gospel implied as to the weakness and temporary nature of the Law, they were hardly likely to be met by the second alternative, that namely of placing those converts in the position of Christian proselytes of the gate. The position of a proselyte of the gate was in point of fact always regarded with disfavour by the stricter of the Jewish doctors. They felt that it implied a shrinking back from the full measure of responsibility involved in the religious profession of the convert, and that (like the position of a catechumen in the Catholic Church) it was satisfactory only when regarded as a state of probation.

But to have received into the Christian pale uncircumcised converts, branding them all the while as half-hearted and imperfect disciples, would have been open not only to the objections which weighed against the profession of a proselyte of the gate, but to one more grave than all arising from the very nature of the

Christian religion in itself. The Eucharist not only implied, by the intimate union which it involved between the Head and the members of the Church, feelings and thoughts to which a line of demarcation drawn through the Church of Christ was essentially and profoundly repugnant;—it presented this repugnance in an outward and tangible form. It compelled those who were partakers of the Christian altar to eat and drink together. If, therefore, a distinction was to be maintained between circumcised and uncircumcised Christians, there must have arisen, wherever Gentile converts accepted the faith of Christ, a double Church, with a double priesthood and a double administration of the sacraments. The unity of the Church would have been broken at the very moment of its announcement as the universal religion of the world.

3. There remained a third course : the absolute emancipation of the Gentile convert from the fetters of the Mosaic Law.

This was, no doubt, the safest as well as the boldest course ; for it was the only course which was consistent with the true spirit of Christianity. But it is also evident that it was only when convinced — and convinced in spite of the strongest national and religious prejudices that this really was the case—that Hebrews would consent to a step which involved an admission that the Law of Moses was no longer necessary to salvation.

Such were the difficulties which prevented the case of Cornelius from becoming the signal of an immediate and large opening of the Church of Christ to the Gentile. They were difficulties exactly such as were sure to be softened by time. St. Peter probably was himself convinced how the great problem must eventually be solved. But, true to his character, he did not force circumstances, he did not press principles to their issue at the risk of dividing the Church, but waited, calm and immoveable, for the further guidance of that Spirit which had led him thus far so surely.

Meantime there burst upon the Church the fury of a new persecution. Agrippa's thirst for popularity cost the life of James the son of Zebedee, and [caused] the arrest of Peter. Delivered by a miracle from prison, he withdrew from the Holy City, leaving James the brother of the Lord in charge of the Church at Jerusalem. The whole Apostolic College, in fact, were now for the first time dispersed; and from this time, it would seem, began that missionary life which is popularly associated with the very name of an Apostle. Of the labours of the greater part we know absolutely nothing. The statement of Eusebius[d], that Thaddæus went to Edessa, Thomas to Parthia, Bartholomew to India, Andrew to the Scythians, almost exhausts our knowledge. But it is certainly remarkable that to this very day we should find in Syria and Kurdistan, in India, Egypt, and Ethiopia, a combination of Jewish usages with orthodox Christian belief which is most easily explained by the supposition that these Churches were established before the great council of Jerusalem had so emphatically discouraged the circumcision of Gentile converts.

To the history of St. Peter himself a deeper interest attaches. The silence of St. Luke with regard to the place of his retreat is in strict accordance with the whole plan of his book; for there was nothing, doubtless, in the apostle's work which was either new in principle or which presented Christianity in contact with a

---

[d] [See Eus. H. E. i. 13, iii. 1, v. 10.]

new class of circumstances. But his silence has been supplied by very various conjectures. The idea that in leaving Jerusalem St. Peter went either to Pontus or to Corinth, may be dismissed at once. It is very doubtful if he visited Pontus at all; it is certain that his visit to Corinth belongs to a later date. Two other destinations, which do not exclude each other, are grouped together in a remarkable passage of Eusebius. It is an entry in his Chronicle[e] under the year A. U. C. 791, the third year of Caius. "The apostle Peter," he says, "after founding the Church of Antioch, sets out for the city of Rome, and there preaches the Gospel. And there he remains as bishop twenty years."

It is certain that this statement is open to very serious criticism.

(1) In the first place, the chronology, which is not consistent with itself, would place the journey of St. Peter to Rome at some date not very far removed from the martyrdom of St. Stephen, and in any case prior to the time when Herod Agrippa became the ruler of Judæa. Such a visit it seems impossible to reconcile with the narrative of St. Luke.

[e] [Eus. Chron. ed. Aucher, ii. 269.]

(2) The foundation of the Church of Antioch by St. Peter seems to be in clear contradiction to the statement of the Acts of the Apostles.

(3) The story of St. Peter having lived at Rome as bishop for twenty years will hardly bear a candid comparison with the Epistles of St. Paul.

Yet a large portion of these objections may be at once conceded, without invalidating more than the circumstantial accuracy of a statement which on closer scrutiny will, I think, be found to be more solid than has sometimes been supposed.

In the first place, the story of a twenty years' episcopate, though in itself untenable, is exactly what would have arisen most naturally in later times, from the fact that the apostle did inaugurate the twenty years by a visit to Rome, and closed them by his martyrdom.

And it is to be observed that the period of *twenty* years, which is evidently meant to include the remainder of the apostle's life, affords incidentally a correction of the faulty chronology of Eusebius. For the martyrdom of St. Peter falls within the years A. D. 64, 65; his emancipation from the prison of Agrippa in the spring of A. D. 44. Correct the chronology by this comparison of dates, and the story falls into its place. It must now be observed that Eusebius, in his Ecclesiastical History, drawn clearly from other sources than those employed for the Chronicle, records a visit of St. Peter to Rome which he places in the reign of Claudius[f]. This tallies exactly with that correction of chronology which the internal evidence of the passage in the Chronicle supplies.

On the whole, then, we may consider that the two passages of Eusebius apply to the same visit, and that the true date to be assigned to it is the year A.D. 44 or 45.

That an event so momentous in the eye of later controversy as the founding of the Church of Rome by the chief of the apostles should be absolutely passed over in the inspired narrative of St. Luke, has appeared to some so strange as to throw entire discredit on the fact. It will appear less strange, indeed, but even more significant to those who have examined closely the structure of the Acts of the Apostles. That book has often, indeed, been regarded as an unmethodical fragment. The incompleteness of the narrative, if viewed as a history of

[f] [Eus. ii. 14.]

the apostles, the sudden change which passes at the close of the twelfth chapter over the persons and scenes of the history, and the abrupt close of the whole, are indeed indications which suggest to the most uncritical reader that he has before him either an unfinished or a most inartistic book. And yet, under this apparent disorder, is concealed a plan as complete, as sustained, as carefully elaborated, as belongs to almost any historical work. The subject of the Acts of the Apostles is the planting of the Church of Christ. How it was originally founded; what were its earliest form and characteristics; what its first difficulties; how it came to be more perfectly organized; how it outgrew the measure of a purely Jewish sect; how, once proclaimed to the Gentiles, it laid hold one by one of the great centres of the Greek and Roman world; how it held on its way from Jerusalem to Samaria, from Samaria to Antioch, to Ephesus, to Corinth, and finally to Rome itself; how it dealt with the varied populations with which it met in its career; how it encountered under the two forms of Judaism and of Gnosticism the germs of all future heresy;—such are the historical questions with which St. Luke deals in the sacred volume of the Acts. He shews us the Church in her majestic advance from Jerusalem to Rome, from the upper chamber of the Eleven to the capital of the Gentile world; and he gives us, in this advance, a prophetic epitome of her history from her first hour to the end.

If in such a narrative as this the visit of St. Peter to Rome finds no place whatever, it can only be that in the mind of the inspired author that visit was not of primary importance in the planting of the Church of Christ. The visit of St. Paul to Rome is of moment; for he plants the greatest of Gentile Churches by the throne of the Gentile world. It is the culminating point of the great apostleship of the Gentiles. But the planting by St. Peter of another Jewish Church, even at Rome itself, is nothing new in principle, nothing which suggests the thought of a mighty future, nothing but the territorial extension of the old Church of the circumcision.

That the Church of Antioch, again, was really founded by St. Peter on his way from Jerusalem to Rome, is a tradition of high antiquity, which there is no reason to question, if only the term *foundation* be understood in that stricter sense in which it was certainly intended. The labours of those dispersed in the persecution of Saul had drawn to the faith of Christ Hellenists residing at Antioch. Barnabas, not yet an apostle, had been sent from Jerusalem to report on the value of their work; but as yet no apostle had visited the infant communion, or conferred those gifts of the laying on of hands without which no Christian community could be truly called a Church. But Antioch, like Rome, owes her place in the history of Christendom to far other events than the probable visit of St. Peter. To that Hellenistic Church, planted in a great city, surrounded by a teeming population of Gentiles, and ministered to by men of the most various origin and sympathies—by Manaen the foster-brother of Herod, by Simeon surnamed the Black, by Lucius of Cyrene, and lastly, by Barnabas and Saul[g],—the question of the conversion of the heathen must have come continually home with a sense of its urgency and its greatness, to which the older Churches of the circumcision were almost of necessity

[g] [Acts xiii. 1.]

strangers. They of Antioch, moreover, had few of the prejudices of the Hebrew; he had few of their opportunities. It might well seem to them that they were called by Providence to be the link between the Jewish and the Gentile world. And thus, as they commended their way to God in special "liturgies and fasts," they received from the Holy Ghost a direct and solemn command, the like of which had never been given to any portion of the Church, to consecrate Barnabas and Saul to the office and work of the apostolate.

The principle laid down in the admission of Cornelius to the Church was now, after the lapse of years, to bear its legitimate fruit. Cyprus, of which Barnabas was a native, was the ground selected for the first missionary work of the two new apostles. And there, before long, the question of preaching to the heathen was brought before them in the broadest and most decisive manner. The fame of their preaching and their miracles spread beyond the synagogues in which alone, as yet, they had taught; and they were sent for by the proconsul Sergius Paulus. Such a case had never occurred before. Cornelius was a heathen, but devout; a proselyte of the gate, incessant in alms and prayer. Paulus was a thorough specimen of the educated heathen of the day, believing in nothing higher than the arts of a Jewish sorcerer.

Even Barnabas, it might seem, was doubtful whether the Gospel should be offered to such a hearer as the proconsul. Saul, "who also is called Paul," took the responsibility upon himself. A miracle approved his boldness; the conversion of the proconsul followed; the last barrier was thrown down which divided the heathen world from the free preaching of the Gospel; and from that hour St. Paul—not his senior and colleague Barnabas—is the chief apostle of the Gentiles.

Fresh advances now followed rapidly. At Antioch in Pisidia the apostles "waxing bold" made the first offer of the Gospel to a whole body of Gentiles. At Lystra, for the first time, the pressure of persecution brings them to a place where no synagogue was to be found; and they find themselves face to face with a rude heathen population, who look upon them as nothing less than gods come down in the shape of men.

Over all the new Churches, Jewish and Gentile alike, they now ordain presbyters, in the full exercise of their own apostolic power. They consider their work as being in no sense tentative or imperfect; it needs no higher sanction, no further apostolic presence, to confer any gift which they were unable to bestow.

Returning to Antioch in Syria, they declared to the Church which had consecrated and sent them forth, the great result of their mission, "how God had opened the door of faith to the Gentiles[h]." At Antioch, the home of their apostleship, where their work was known and their authority fully owned, they remained to carry out the principles which their great mission had established, and to gather round the old Hellenistic nucleus a great Gentile Church.

There, on the banks of the Orontes, did Christianity lay hold for the first time of the mixed population of one of the great cities of the Empire, and found as it were a capital of her

[h] Acts xiv. 27. It is hard to see what meaning this can bear if Ἕλληνας be read in xi. 20, or, in other words, Antioch be supposed to be already a Gentile Church, On the other hand, the studied parallelism of expression between this verse and xi. 18 shews how St. Luke would have us understand that the case of Cornelius really involved the principle.

own in the heart of the heathen world. Antioch remained for many years the centre of Gentile Christendom. It was here that the complications were first felt between Jewish and Gentile converts, which were destined to be so painfully conspicuous in the history of the early Church.

CHAPTER III.

The Council of Jerusalem.

WHILE the young Church of Antioch had thus become the source of the apostleship of the Gentiles and the capital of Gentile Christendom, the mother Church of Jerusalem continued to be the centre of that severe and unbending Hebraism which seems, as a rule, to have marked the converted Pharisee. None indeed desired more earnestly the conversion of the Gentile world, but they desired it upon condition of a close continuity with the religious past of their nation; they desired that the Gospel should be a more glorious expansion of the Law, giving to its disciples a new strength to observe the Divine precepts, a clearer and keener vision of the glory of the Divine promises. They looked upon the Mosaic Law as something perfect and unchangeable; upon circumcision as the perpetual rite of admission into covenant with God.

Therefore when the news came down that a large Gentile Church was rapidly arising at Antioch, and that under the hands of men who might well seem to have usurped the name and office of apostles;—when they found, moreover, that no word was being said which would imply that these converts from heathenism were bound either to circumcision or to the observance of the Mosaic Law,—they took alarm at a movement so entirely at variance with their ideas of the relation of Christianity to the law of the ancient covenant. They came down to Antioch; they declared with the authority of teachers from the mother Church of Christendom, that no Christian whatever was exempt from the rite of circumcision. They were resisted by Paul and Barnabas. The liberty of the Gentile Church was too weighty a point to be surrendered even for the sake of peace. And thus for the first time was the Church of Christ divided and her teachers openly arrayed in hostile controversy.

Unable to agree, they resolved to submit the question to the decision of the apostles and presbyters at Jerusalem, and representatives of both parties were accordingly sent up by the Church to attend at Jerusalem the deliberations of this the first Christian Council. St. Paul, chosen with Barnabas to be the exponent of their common views, went up with a reluctance which was only overcome by the guidance of a special revelation[a].

There was, indeed, mixed up with the question of the circumcision of Gentile converts, another more personal to himself, which he may well have hesitated to submit to any human judgment—the validity of his own call to the apostolic office. That which had been the direct act of the Spirit, it might seem to be a profanation to submit to the revision even of apostles. That power which it was necessary for him to uphold in all its integrity and independence, might seem likely to be compromised if it should be brought in any way before the tribunal of the Church, instead of standing simply upon the fiat of the Divine Will.

The revelation which removed his scruples directed, doubtless, the course of action which he took. When, therefore, he went up, in

[a] [Gal. ii. 2.]

obedience to the Divine command, his first care was to obtain, in a private conference with a few of the chief apostles, a recognition of the validity of his own apostolic character. Armed with this recognition he appeared in the Council to plead, as the apostle of the Gentiles, the cause of Gentile liberty. The decision, if not perhaps such as St. Paul himself would have penned, conceded the great principle that circumcision and the Law of Moses were not to bind the Gentile converts to Christ. In other respects the regard for Jewish prejudices, and the true Christian unwillingness to wound a weaker brother, gave to the decree an unmistakeable tone of compromise.

Not only were the feelings of the Jews—upon whose weekly worship at the synagogue the Gentile Christians were still in the habit of attending—to be consulted by the command that all should abstain "from meats offered to idols, and from blood, and from things strangled, and from fornication," but the really important question, which had touched men so keenly at the time of the conversion of Cornelius, and which had still continued to embarrass the action of the Church of Jerusalem—the question, namely, whether Jewish Christians should be expected to eat and to drink with men uncircumcised,—this question, which might seem to threaten the very unity of the Church of Christ, was left untouched by the decree. Most wisely, no doubt; for we shall soon see how little the Church was ripe for so decisive a measure.

Apart from the matter of the decree, there is more than one thing noticeable in the meeting of the Council of Jerusalem. More than two centuries must elapse before another Council assembles, of the constitution and acts of which we have a full and authentic narrative. This stands, as it were, raised on a pedestal of honour, a solitary record of the very earliest mode of holding Councils of the Church.

First, then, it is observable that the president of the Council is not St. Peter, but St. James. Before the dispersion of the Twelve, they had placed St. James, the brother of our Lord, in charge of the Church of Jerusalem, Eminent as he was by character, illustrious from his near connexion with our Lord according to the flesh, he was yet not one of those to whom He had committed the general government of the Church. Nor does he ever occupy, except at

Jerusalem, that foremost place in which he here appears. At Jerusalem, however, he always stands the first. He presides at the Council; he is named by St. Paul in connexion with the Council before St. Peter and St. John; he appears again as presiding when the Church of Jerusalem met to receive St. Paul immediately before his imprisonment.

We have therefore a remarkable admission, in this presidency of St. James, of the principle of local rank and authority in the hierarchy of the Christian Church. Less than an apostle elsewhere, in Jerusalem St. James takes precedence of the very chief of the Twelve.

Of the constitution of the Council the narrative appears at first sight to give two different accounts. In two passages it speaks of the apostles and the presbyters; in three it implies the presence or the assent of the entire Church. The discrepancy, a fruitful source of controversy, disappears on a careful reading.

We are told by St. Luke, first that the appeal of the Church of Antioch was made to the apostles and presbyters; next, that the apostles and presbyters came together to deliberate. After much discussion, the weighty words of

St. Peter obtained a hearing for the apostles Barnabas and Paul, and we are told that "the whole multitude" kept silence, to receive the account of their doings among the Gentiles. The discussion is then closed, and the final opinion of the Council expressed by St. James. Finally, the decretal letter of the Council runs in the name of the apostles, and presbyters, and brethren; and the delegates charged with their delivery are commissioned by the apostles and presbyters "with the whole Church." The only fair inference is that the discussion was confined to the apostles and presbyters, but that that discussion was public in the face of the Church, and the decision approved by the whole body of the brethren, who also were consulted as to the fittest means of communicating that decision when approved.

Finally, it is remarkable how emphatically the Council claims for its decisions the sanction of the Holy Spirit. "It seemed good to the Holy Ghost and to us" are, so to speak, the enacting words of a Council which had shared to the full in the heat and vehemence of debate, and whose final decree bears visible marks of the conflict of individual opinions, and of that spirit of compromise which we are wont to regard as one of the surest marks of the infirmity of human counsels. And if only too often in the later Councils of the Church the play of human passion and the balance of party intrigue have found too large a scope, it may yet be that their decrees repose upon a basis which the passion and the weakness of men have no power to disturb.

The consequences of the decrees of Jerusalem, their rejection, their acceptance, their modification and expansion, and the relations which under their influences arose between the Jewish and Gentile members of the one Church of Christ, colour the whole history of the later Apostolic age.

1. Nothing more strikingly illustrates the manner in which the most absolute devotion to the one common faith, and to the one sacred cause of Christ, can consist with the free play of individual character, and even with divergence of opinion, than the treatment of these decrees by the most eminent of the apostles themselves.

When after the Council St. Peter went down to Antioch, he acted in the spirit of his own words to the Council;—he acknowledged the full equality of Jew and Gentile in Christ; he broke through the barrier of ceremonial pollution, and ate and drank with the Gentile members of the Church. Yet it is evident that he was drawn only gradually, and as it were reluctantly, to accept this bold position. It is doubly interesting from this point of view to compare the earlier testimony of St. Peter, as addressed to Cornelius and his fellows, both with his own words in the Council and with the first recorded preaching of St. Paul. St. Peter when speaking to Cornelius, like St. Paul to the Pisidians of Antioch, places before his hearers the great fact of the Gospel—the forgiveness of sins through Jesus: but the one points alone to the moral side of Christianity, and to the promise of forgiveness through our Judge; the other touches on the largeness of the Divine grace, and contrasts it, for the first time in the records of Christian preaching, with the weakness and inefficacy of the Law. How remarkable is it, after this comparison of the earlier teaching of the two, to hear St. Peter in the Council, fresh from his conference with St. Paul, adopting the language of him whom he had but now accepted as his colleague, and declaring in no uncertain terms that the Law of Moses was a yoke "which neither our fathers nor we were able to bear!" We seem here to see the teaching of St. Peter visibly broadening in its contact with the bolder spirit of St. Paul. We see him next at Antioch carrying out this bolder tone into free communion with the Gentiles. And yet, with so unsteady a grasp did he hold these larger principles, that "when certain came from James[b]," he yielded to the influence of their scruples, and abstained from the intercourse which before he had gladly admitted. He fell into the temptation; but it was only to learn by his fall, and to fix its great lesson irrevocably in his heart for ever. The strong personality of Cephas is not merged in the inspiration of the apostle. And his was not, like St. Paul's, a mind which makes a principle its own, and tries it in all its bearings by the power of an intellectual foresight. He was rather one of those whose great schoolmaster is a life in the light of God; who treasure up their experiences; who learn *deeply* by their failures, and who broaden and deepen

[b] [Gal. ii. 12.]

year by year the irregular channels of a massive and thoughtful character.

Of St. James there is every reason to believe that he remained to the last a severe and ascetic observer of the Mosaic Law. The position which he occupies in the pages of Hegesippus[c] and the pseudo-Clementine Homilies is so far as this in complete accordance with the language he addressed to St. Paul in the presence of the Church of Jerusalem[d]. He speaks of the many myriads of Jews who believed in Christ, as all zealous for the Law. He identifies himself completely with their feelings, and dwells on the great concession made to the Gentile converts as demanding in return a full and public acknowledgment of the propriety of the Jewish practice.

Unlike St. Peter, who touched with his varied sympathies both the great sections of the Church, St. James stands forward as the head of the strictly Jewish party; of those, that is, who while perfectly loyal to the decree of the Council of Jerusalem, adhered for themselves to the observance of the Mosaic Law, and avoided, it would seem, such intercourse

[c] [Eus. ii. 23.] [d] [Acts xxi. 20.]

with uncircumcised converts as would have been at variance with their life as Jews before their conversion to Christianity.

The little that we know, as regards these questions, of St. John, would lead us to ascribe to him a less decided leaning in the same general direction. It may suffice, for the moment, to observe that in the Apocalypse[e] he groups together the eating things sacrificed to idols, and committing fornication, as a holding of the doctrine of Balaam. The practices are condemned, as they were at the Council of Jerusalem; and the condemnation is rested in either case upon grounds which are not distinctively Christian.

In marked and even startling contrast to the three "pillars" of the Church, stands the language and the conduct of the great Apostle of the Gentiles. He circumcises, and he refuses to circumcise; he observes and he neglects the Law; he forbids and he permits the eating things offered to idols, with an unfettered freedom, with a total absence of allusion to the solemn decree of the Council, which might raise a question, if such a question were pos-

[e] [Rev. ii. 14.]

sible, whether St. Paul could ever have been a consenting party to the decree. He carefully avoids all mention of it even in that Epistle to the Galatians in which he travels exactly over the ground which it covers, and mentions the very visit to Jerusalem which was occasioned by the summoning of the Council. He everywhere implies that he considers the restrictive clauses of the decree, not as a permanent command, but as a local and temporary compromise.

The motive to a line of conduct so strongly contrasted with the measured position of the great apostles of the circumcision is to be found perhaps, in part, in the strong intellectual bias which leads him continually back from the particular instance, to the broad principle which underlies it; in part, in the peculiar position which he occupied as the special Apostle of the Gentiles.

The circumstances which at Antioch had forced St. Peter to break through his Jewish rules, and to eat and drink with Gentiles, were to St. Paul not an occasional event, but the normal condition of his life. He was in incessant charge of Churches in which the Jewish and Gentile elements were variously mixed together. If they could not be brought to eat and drink together, the unity of the Church would be shaken to its very foundation. His task was therefore to prevail upon the mass of Jewish Christians to take, upon personal conviction, the course which had cost St. Peter an effort, which St. James himself had declined, and which the Council of Jerusalem had distinctly refused to decree. And this was alone possible by explaining to its depths the relations which existed between the old and the new covenants; by shewing to the Jew how little worth was the distinctive character on which he prided himself so highly; by shewing to the Gentile, on the other hand, how large was the debt of honour and of gratitude which was due to that people to whom had been committed "the keeping of the oracles of God [f]," and the religious training of the world; how full was the allowance to be made for the weak conscience, which the bias of ceremonial discipline had made timid in the matter of meat and drinks [g].

2. Thus within the narrow circle of the chiefs

[f] [Rom. iii. 2.]   [g] [Rom. xiv. 2 seq.; 1 Cor. viii. 12.]

of the early Church there was included every shade of opinion as to the keeping of the Mosaic Law, consistent with allegiance to the apostolic Council. It cannot be matter for surprise if, beyond that circle, the divergence was even wider, and if even the cautious decision of the Council became the signal for the formation of a Judaizing party which rejected its authority, which held up St. James as the pattern of the Christian life, and pursued with an undying hatred the labours and the memory of St. Paul. Their influence was deep and lasting. Foiled at Antioch, they turned aside to the remoter Churches which had been founded by St. Paul in his first missionary journey. We find from the Epistle to the Galatians that in the Churches of that province they had only formed a party. They began their work by denying the apostolic authority of St. Paul. They probably represented his consecration as the unauthorized act of the secondary Church of Antioch, unknown to the Twelve, who held a different language and taught another doctrine.

Here, as elsewhere, they must have disallowed the authority of the Council of Jerusalem; and in this probably, and in that which it involved, consisted the sum of their doctrinal errors. There is nothing in the Epistle to the Galatians which suggests that they otherwise fell short of the standard of the apostolic teaching.

The Epistle to the Romans gives us one slight indication of their presence[h]; and in the Church of Corinth they appear to have obtained a footing as one of the many parties which distracted the unity of that remarkable and important Church. The Corinthians, who would naturally be prone to seize with Greek subtlety the shades of intellectual difference which divided from each other the great teachers of Christianity, and to realize but imperfectly the difference between a Saviour and a teacher, between Christ and Paul, were visited in the absence of their founder by men who impugned his apostolic authority and questioned the integrity of his doctrine. Some of these appealed to St. Peter, as the unquestioned chief of the Twelve; others possibly to St. James, as preserving unadulterated the pure teaching of the Lord; and thus the Church was broken up into adherents of Paul, of Apollos, of Cephas, of Christ. But, however strongly the apostle is compelled to write of the

[h] [Rom. xvi. 17.]

conduct of these false apostles, there is still no indication that they brought with them any other teaching than that which they had already introduced into the Galatian Church.

In the Epistle to the Colossians we catch the first indication of a certain change of position. No sect or party can long exist on a basis of pure negation. The Judaizing teachers finding, no doubt, the influence of this common law, began to develop a theosophic teaching of their own, which the apostle describes as a "philosophy and vain deceit, after the tradition of men[1]." We further learn that this teaching consisted not only in the stress laid on the observance of holy days, and new moons, and Sabbaths, in common with the earlier Judaism, but in a worshipping of angels, a mystic teaching on the subject of the unseen world, and a rigidly ascetic discipline, all which were calculated, in the judgment of the apostle, to draw men away from Christ, and to lead them especially to lose sight of their sacramental union with Him.

The Pastoral Epistles exhibit, apparently, a still further development in the same direction. For we find there not only the "Jewish fables

[1] [Col. ii. 8.]

and commandments of men," "the profane and old wives' fables," the "endless genealogies" of angels and powers, which seem to be pointed to in the earlier Epistle to the Colossians; but we also find, for the first time, mention of the prohibition of marriage, and the memorable name of Gnosis, which suggests the incipient union of Judaism with another class of errors[k].

We are brought by these notices of the Judaizing party of the Church almost to the eve of the taking of Jerusalem. That event, following quickly on the deaths of St. Peter, St. Paul, and St. James, seems to form the natural close of the earlier apostolic age. Its full importance to the Church, and especially to the Jewish portion of it, we shall be able better to understand when we have before us more completely the extent and character of the earlier apostolic work.

[k] [Tit. i. 14; 1 Tim. iv. 7; i. 4; iv. 3; vi. 20.]

CHAPTER IV.

St. Paul and the elder Apostles.

OF the extent of the Church at the time of the Council of Jerusalem we possess no complete information. But the years which had elapsed since the persecution of Herod had been fruitful of apostolic labour, and at all the chief centres of the Jewish dispersion there were probably by this time Churches of more or less importance; as, for instance, at Rome, Alexandria, and Edessa. But what is of really more importance, is the negative knowledge that there were as yet no Gentile communities beyond the limits of St. Paul's missionary labours. A few Churches in Syria, Cyprus, and Asia Minor complete the short list. In the heart of the Gentile world, the great centres of Greek and Roman civilization, Christianity was hardly known—known perhaps only at Rome, as the belief of the last and most obscure of Jewish sects.

The Council was followed by an immediate step in advance. It was one of the first cares of St. Paul to visit once more the Churches he had planted in Cilicia and Pisidia, and to deliver into their hands the apostolic letter. When he had fulfilled his task, his intention was to complete the circuit of Asia Minor; but the "Spirit suffered him not[a]." By the special direction of God he crossed over into Europe; and we feel as we cross with him how entirely the scene is changed, and how natural was the reluctance of the Jew, apostle of the Gentiles though he was, to encounter the difficulties of a work in many respects so new; how natural the shrinking of the Oriental, even with all his Hellenistic training, from confronting the full tide of Western thought, and from adapting himself to the strangeness of Western manners. The stronger hold of Rome, the thinner ranks and weaker influence of Judaism, strike us at once. Passing by many minor details, the accusation at Philippi of teaching a *religio non licita*, at Thessalonica of teaching "contrary to the decrees

[a] [Acts xvi. 7.]

of Cæsar," the appeal of St. Paul to his citizenship, are all indications of the presence and power of Roman influence and manners. The want of any regular synagogue at an important place like Philippi, the subsequent selection of Thessalonica as the place " where was *the*[b] synagogue of the Jews," mark the scarcity of Jews, while the pointed expression "being Jews" appears to suggest the existence of a popular prejudice against them. It is significant, again, of the state of religion among these few Jews, that women only are spoken of as resorting to the place of prayer at Philippi; that at Thessalonica the "chief women" seem to have formed the most important section among the Jewish converts; and that the presence of not a few men among the converts at Berœa is the subject of especial remark.

Nothing could be less hopeful to a missionary who, like St. Paul, had found hitherto the scene of his first labours and the nucleus of his converts in the congregation of the synagogues. The people were in fact peculiarly hard of access. But the same Providence which directed the apparently unpromising step of leaving Asia for

[b] [Acts xvii. 1: ἡ συναγωγή.]

Europe, prepared a new opening adapted to the altered circumstances. The casting out of the spirit of divination at Philippi, the imprisonment, the miracle of release, formed a chain of events which led to the preaching of the Gospel to the Gentiles. As the Epistle of St. Paul witnesses, the Church of Philippi became predominantly a Gentile Church: and in the scene of his deep trials and anxieties in this "beginning of the Gospel^c" there grew up a body of disciples attached to him by ties of the warmest personal affection.

With the visit of St. Paul to Athens we see Christianity in contact, for the first time, with the prevailing philosophy of the West. The spirit of St. Paul was stirred within him when he found himself in the capital of intellectual heathenism. He can no longer confine himself to his preachings in the Jewish synagogue; he has a word even for the intellectual triflers of the agora.

To the historian of the Church his speech on the Areopagus possesses this peculiar interest—that in it are indicated, with singular clearness and power, the leading points of contact and of

^c [Phil. iv. 15.]

difference between the religion of Christ and the intellectual power of that great empire with which during three centuries its mighty struggle was to continue.

Admitting the fitness of that reverence for the powers of the unseen world[d] which had crowded Athens with the monuments of religious splendour; admitting no less the apparently conflicting doctrines of Epicurean and of Stoic, that mankind were of one blood; he harmonizes the two by a teaching in some respects entirely new, in others completely alien to the mind of the heathen world. If the doctrine of a Creator was long known to the Jews, the idea of the unity of all history, and of the rise and fall of nations as parts of a single Divine plan, was propounded for the first time, in all the freshness of its originality, to the feeble imitators who claimed to be the inheritors of Greek philosophy. But it was no point of speculative difference, however momentous, that repelled the educated heathen. Where Christianity parted from unchristian philosophy, then as ever, was on the ground of the supernatural. When St. Paul spoke of the resurrection, Athens

[d] [Acts xvii. 22.]

would listen no longer. Paul passed from among them. On intellectual Athens he scarcely made an impression: in luxurious and licentious Corinth he planted one of the foremost of Christian Churches.

The foundation of the Church of Corinth was, in fact, the great result of the second journey of St. Paul. In it he was compelled by Jewish hostility to withdraw altogether from the synagogue, and to establish for the first time a place of separate Christian worship; in it was felt, for the first time, the influence of the Greek Schools, the fruitful source of division; in it was conspicuous the taint of foul impurity, derived from heathen profligacy. And yet, with every drawback, with abounding elements of evil, the Church of Corinth became to Greece what Antioch had been to Syria, what Ephesus afterwards became to the whole of Asia Minor; it became the Christian capital of the most cultivated country of the world.

As the crowning event of St. Paul's first and second journeys had been the foundation of the Gentile Churches of Antioch and of Corinth, so that of the third journey is the establishment, if not strictly the foundation, of the yet greater

Church of Ephesus. For it is not to the hurried visit of St. Paul at the close of his second journey that we turn as the true date of its planting, but rather to the long stay of two years and upwards[e] which it was almost his earliest care to make on his return back from Jerusalem. And that long stay was in more respects than one a period of advance in the career of the great apostle.

Ephesus was eminently a religious city. The popular idolatry, enshrined in unusual splendour, vied with the arts of magic in engrossing the affection of the people, whose moral sense they alike outraged and degraded. In the conflict with these baser powers, the gifts of the Spirit appear to have shone out in more than their common splendour. Miracles of unusual power were wrought by the hands of St. Paul; the counterfeit exorcism of the sons of Sceva was put to public shame; the gulph which separated the works of the Spirit from the arts of the sorcerer was made clear to the eye of every one; and the taint of magic, which had hitherto clung even to the infant Church, was wiped away in a costly confession. But it is not only

[e] [Acts xix. 10, 22.]

in the splendour of his success at Ephesus, won, as were his greatest successes, in the midst of intense personal suffering, that we perceive the peculiar greatness of this period of the apostolic life of St. Paul. The same singular power extends itself to his writings; and from Ephesus were written the four palmary Epistles to the Corinthians, the Galatians, and the Romans. And not only so: but it is evident that to the eye of St. Paul the horizon of the Church has widened. The new Gentile Churches of Corinth and of Ephesus have assumed an importance and displayed a spiritual power which has reacted upon the apostle himself. He no longer writes in the tone of the Epistles to the Thessalonians, of the second coming of the Lord as of an event which for want as it were of perspective seems to overhang the future of the Christian Church; but he speaks for the first time of Rome—he looks forward to the conquest of the world. The very apostle whom it required a vision to lead over into Europe is flushed as it were with victory, and can rest satisfied with no goal for his career but the capital of the world itself.

It is at that crowning point of his apostleship

—at the visit to Rome, for which he had longed so earnestly—that St. Luke closes the history which has been our constant guide; and the last years of Paul's life are involved in much obscurity. It may, however, be received as sufficiently certain that he was released from his imprisonment at Rome, and that he fulfilled the intention he had expressed of making a journey to Spain. From thence he returned eastward, and revisited the Churches of Proconsular Asia and of Greece. It is probable that, as he intended[f], he went to Nicopolis to winter, and that there he was arrested and brought to Rome as a Christian leader, on the charge of being concerned in the burning of the city.

Certain it is that in the same persecution by Nero, St. Peter and St. Paul were both martyred at Rome. A late tradition has recorded that the very same day closed the career of the two great apostles. The imagination loves to give precision to a coincidence so striking as the simultaneous martyrdom of the two pillars of the Jewish and Gentile Church. The two streams, so slow at first to mingle, might seem

[f] [Tit. iii. 12.]

to be blended in their blood. They might seem not less to have met at last in Rome, and to have pointed her out as the natural capital of Christendom. So at least it would seem to Roman eyes, when circumstances, which we will not forestall, had given her an acknowledged primacy among the Churches of the world.

This portion of the history cannot be concluded without some consideration of the relation in which the apostles stood to each other as teachers and governors of the Church. The most opposite opinions have, in fact, obtained upon this important point. While some writers have spoken as if they moved, like parts of one great machine, with undeviating precision towards one grand object, exhibiting no shade of difference in doctrine, and but little in tone of character; others have spoken of the discipline and theology of the Church as worked out into its ultimate shape, far in the second century, by the late and difficult pacification of a stormy conflict of opinion in which the apostles of Christ were the chiefs of opposing camps.

The first opinion certainly derives no sanction from antiquity, and is in fact the product of a modern theory of inspiration. The second is to be found, under one form, in the pseudo-Clementine Homilies, a heretical work of which we shall hereafter have occasion to speak again, and which appeared soon after the middle of the second century. It is there maintained that the earliest Church had two sets of doctrine, an exoteric and a secret; and that St. Peter and St. James, finding it vain to preserve the exoteric teaching free from the corruptions of St. Paul and his school, handed down a secret lore to be divulged when the times should be more prepared for its reception, and that it was in fact so published early in the second century. That secret doctrine is a modification of the great Ebionitic heresy; by which our Lord was regarded as the human Messiah of the Jews, and as the greatest of all the prophets; but with express denial of His Divine Nature and Kingdom.

In modern times this theory has assumed a simpler form. The difficult machinery of an open and a secret teaching has disappeared from view; but it has been maintained that the teaching of the original apostles was Ebionitic or humanitarian, and that to St. Paul primarily is due the higher theology which we now receive as Catholic. The generic resemblance between the theories of the pseudo-Clement and of Baur is one of the most suggestive of the many points of likeness between the controversies of the second and the nineteenth century. The differences in detail are at the same time significant; for it is evident that the Clementine writer found a difficulty in harmonizing his position with known and notorious facts, which is unfelt by his modern successor; while the modern feels, not less acutely, the critical absurdity of the contrivance by which the difficulty is evaded. They may be left to comment on each other. It is obvious that either view is really inconsistent with acknowledging, I will not say the inspiration, but the genuineness of the Gospel of St. John.

In a work which, like the present, assumes the exactness of the New Testament Canon, the discussion of such opinions is beyond our province. But it does concern us to point out that in their modern shape they ultimately rest upon a faulty treatment of history, which has led in countless instances to conclusions, perhaps less extravagant, but hardly less untrue. Such views, in fact, are only possible where the history of doctrine is extensively studied apart from the general history of the Church; and they stand as a warning against all that handling of history which reduces it to a branch of literary criticism. The relations in which the apostles actually stood to each other are in fact to be ascertained far less by framing a theology out of the extant writings of each, than by considering how they must have been affected by the mode of their training and their appointment, by the nature of their powers, and by the links which bound together the society of which they were the rulers. In point of fact the writings even of St. Paul and St. John are inadequate to express their whole theology. Each has contributed to the Canon not his whole system, but that special side of his teaching of which he seemed to the Holy Spirit to be the most appropriate organ; and the account of their opinions, based simply on an analysis of their writings, however perfect and however free from colouring such an analysis may be, must always exaggerate what is distinctive of the individual, and throw into the shade what belongs to the Christian and the apostle.

It must never [g], then, be forgotten how entirely the life of the early Church centred round the sacred Person of its Lord. In Him they were an unbroken brotherhood "of one heart and of one soul," extending itself step by step, before the apostleship of St. Paul, to the Hellenist, to the Samaritan, to the uncircumcised eunuch, to the Roman centurion. From Him was derived the authority of that government of the one Church, which for twelve years at least the apostles exercised together as a sacred college at Jerusalem. Of Him witnessed those Gospel narratives, to the very early existence of which our synoptical Gospels bear so sure a testimony. To Him, lastly, was the Church most closely united by a common worship, and above all, by the sacraments, the full significance of which is assuredly no after-revelation, for it is implied, certainly as regards the Eucharist, in the founding words of the Lord.

Believing in their Master as Divine, conscious of being endued with a Divine power, and of

---

[g] "To be put more fully—Apostles had been disciples.—The *"pillars"* exclusive witnesses of Transfiguration, &c.—Care to direct the two guiding minds.—Primacy of St. Peter.—Unity."—[*Note in pencil in MS.*]

acting under a Divine commission, the apostles were not the disciples of a great teacher, each urging forward his principles to conclusions not imagined by their common master; but servants of a common Lord, from whose Divine Spirit they sought their daily guidance, and to whose Divine command they bowed in rejoicing reverence.

Yet when all this has been admitted in all its full significance, it does not lead us to regard the apostles as mechanical agents whose intellect and heart and will have lost their personality in the overpowering greatness of the influence under which they worked. Rather, as free-will itself is the crowning work of creation, the crowning work of man's restoration by grace is to restore and enlarge the freedom of his enfeebled will. If studied aright, no characters in history exhibit a more vigorous individuality; none, rather, embody with greater vividness the great types of human character— it may be added, of Christian theology—than the chief apostles of the Lord.

Nor is it less to be allowed that the theology of the apostles grew, like their characters, by the light of a varied experience. Just as in the after-history of the Church contact with the successive movements of human opinion and society elicited with increasing distinctness the consciousness and the expression of her doctrines, so, in a far higher degree, was this the case in the apostolic age. The conversion of Cornelius and the Council of Jerusalem were steps in advance, as real and yet more weighty than the Council of Nicæa itself; the influence of St. Paul as a theologian as real and yet more mighty than that of St. Chrysostom or St. Augustine. But it is the nature of such a growth that the teaching in which it is presented gives on a superficial view an altogether exaggerated idea of its real character and extent. It lies, in truth, in the constitution of the human mind that great principles are always slow to work themselves out to their conclusions; and that great truths, however firmly accepted, are slow to assume in the mind such a distinctness of outline as admits of their presentation in all their fulness to the minds of others.

From this condition of humanity the apostles were not exempted. The Gospels abound in instances of their slowness to comprehend the bearing of their Lord's teaching, or to draw from it the most immediate and necessary inferences. The Acts of the Apostles witness to the continuance, in a degree, of the same human slowness, even after the day of Pentecost; and on this ground alone we might well be led to understand the immensity of the interval, in point of doctrinal distinctness, which divides the Pentecostal teaching of St. Peter from the final words of St. John. And it is most worthy of note, from this point of view, that the very apostle who drank most deeply of the spiritual teaching of our Lord, and whose theology is confessedly the deepest and most unearthly of all, should have been the last to commit to writing the teaching with which he was peculiarly charged. It would seem as if those profoundly spiritual portions of our blessed Lord's discourses which he has transmitted to us, had made comparatively but a light impression on the minds of His other hearers. While they had in a manner blasted him with excess of light, they had left him so dazzled and perplexed that he who in the lifetime of his Lord was at once the apostle of His love and the Son of Thunder, played comparatively but a secondary part in the early planting of the Church, and only emerged into the fulness of his apostolic greatness when years of adoring meditation had removed every mist from the image of that Divine Friend, on whose breast he had leant at supper, and at the feet of whose glory he fell as one dead.

If, then, the lessons imparted by our Lord needed thus to be matured in the hearts of His apostles before they could be produced in all the clearness of their outline, we can see one reason for that absence of higher teaching as to the sacred Person of Christ which so clearly marks the first chapters of the Acts.

But there is another reason, of which we find the impress, even in an exaggerated form, upon all the missionary work of the early Church. The reticence which shrouded the holiest Christian mysteries from the knowledge of those who were likely only to dishonour them, is blended with the prudence which presents to the mind of each enquirer that side of the truth which would be likely to make the first and most decisive impression upon him. And of this reserve and this prudence we find abundant traces not only in the earlier chapters of the Acts

—in which we are by some supposed to read the pre-Pauline theology of the Church—but also in those later chapters which are dedicated almost wholly to the work of St. Paul himself. If we had to look to the Acts of the Apostles alone, we should form almost as inadequate an impression of the theology of St. Paul from the concluding chapters of the book as we should of the theology of St. Peter from the earlier.

It may well seem amazing that any one could rise from the perusal of the Gospel narrative and believe that the first twelve chapters contain an adequate account of the theology of the chief of those chosen Twelve, to whom the Lord had taught, without veil or parable, the mysteries of the kingdom of heaven; to whom He had foretold His sufferings and His resurrection; in whose presence He had cast out devils and had raised the dead; with whom He instituted the sacrament of His body and blood; and to whom He had left as a last command, that they should baptize in the name of the Father, the Son, and the Holy Ghost.

The complete failure of the attempt to elicit from the early chapters of the Acts a body of primitive theology may well make us cautious in the application of a similar method to the comparative teaching of the apostles. If doctrines of cardinal importance, which we know to have been held by the very earliest Christians, yet fail to appear in a narrative like that of the Acts, what reasonable expectation can we form of extracting from the brief Epistles of St. Peter and St. James the whole theology of these two apostolic leaders? It is evident, indeed, that any negative argument from the omission of particular doctrines is powerless when weighed in the balance against the considerations to be derived from the general position of the apostles and Church of Christ; and that even when they speak of facts and doctrines which are dwelt upon by other apostles in apparently divergent language, their differences are to be estimated, if the meaning of their words is doubtful, by what we know from other sources of the relation of the apostles to each other, not only as disciples of the same Divine Master, but partakers of a common gift of apostleship, and as fellow-rulers of a Church which bound its meanest members together by a tie more close than brotherhood.

Yet, none the less, the work of Christ was done, among apostles as among their successors, by men of very various character; and His doctrine was apprehended by them from points of view as various.

CHAPTER V.

The Nature of the Apostolic Church.

AT the martyr-tombs of the two great apostles, on the eve of the destruction of Jerusalem, we may pause for a moment in the rapid course of our history to answer, if possible, some few of the more momentous questions which are suggested by the first years of the Church.

We have watched her victorious advance from the upper chamber of Jerusalem to the heart of imperial Rome; but we have seen her rather in her conquests, or in her relations to the external world, than in her own inner being. We have passed over as yet in silence, or touched but very lightly, the inevitable enquiry as to the nature of the Church itself, as to the links by which it was sustained in unity and matchless power, as to the relations which existed within her between the governors and the governed, and between the individual members of the governing Apostolic College.

With immediate reference to the question of government, there are perhaps two points in the primitive conception of the Church which are of fundamental importance.

1. That the idea of the Church, *as a permanent and universal institution*, was formed only by degrees.

It has been almost like a law of the Church's being, that in times of deep religious fervour and emotion a belief should be widely diffused of the immediate coming of the Lord; and that such was emphatically the belief of the apostolic age appears from the New Testament to be abundantly clear. The blending of the two events, the taking of Jerusalem and the second coming of the Lord, in the twenty-fourth chapter of St. Matthew; the conduct of the first Thessalonian Christians, the answer of St. Paul to them, the closing words of the Apocalypse, with other minor indications,—are evidence to a fact which would perhaps never have been doubted but for the undue inferences which have sometimes been drawn from it. It was only by slow degrees, and by the light of the Holy Spirit upon an ever-widening experience, that the first disciples learned that the preaching of the

Gospel among all nations, which was to precede their Lord's return, was something of which the preaching of the day of Pentecost was only the type and foretaste. They regarded the sacred brotherhood in[a]   *   *   *   *

First, perhaps, the martyrdom of St. James, breaking the charmed circle of their twelve apostolic chiefs, then the apostleship of St. Paul and Barnabas, then the growth of the Gentile Church, the martyrdom of the two great apostles at Rome, the destruction of the Holy City,—all were so many steps by which the Church was awakened to a full and lively consciousness that it was destined to outlive the space of human life, and to play a durable part in the history of the world. And side by side with the belief in the permanence of the Church grew up the belief in its universality. She admitted the Gentile to full and equal communion, and found as she extended her vision into the distant future, that she had new worlds to conquer. And growing thus surely, but slowly, to the sense of her immense and lasting work, she would

---

[a] [Here a page is wanting in the MS. A few words in pencil seem to indicate its subject: " Expecting Christ's return.—The kingdom to Israel, &c.—Waiting at Jerusalem."]

nturally grow also as surely and as slowly to the full formation of that government which was needed, not only for her earliest work, but to replace apostles as they were removed by the hand of death, or to assist them in the care of Churches which were fast outgrowing their powers of personal supervision. To suppose, indeed, that it was otherwise is to assume the occurrence of a miracle, wholly without evidence, and contrary to the analogy of the common course of revelation and of the rest of the Church's history.

2. But, secondly, however rudimentary the idea of the Church may have been in the first years of its existence, whether as to the permanence or the universality of its purpose; however afterwards it was elaborated, expanded, modified,—by the Church upon earth the first disciples always understood an union of man to man in a visible and organic society.

They did not of course deny the presence of unfaithful members within the visible Church, but it was contrary to their mode of thought to speak of the truly faithful as of an invisible Church. Still less, of course, could they have formed the idea of an invisible Church consisting of those who, however severed from communion with each other upon earth, are united together by the love of their common Lord. Historically indeed, this conception, so familiar to modern thought, had its origin, or at least its full definition, in the polemical exigencies of the continental Protestants of the sixteenth and seventeenth centuries; who when pressed by Romanists with the inconsistency between their position and the belief in One Catholic Church, replied that they believed the Catholic Church to be invisible, and to be in fact the company of God's elect. It is obvious, however, that such a definition, whatever it may be worth, would never have led to the placing of One Catholic Church among the primary objects of the Christian faith; and that, arising as it did out of the failure of external unity, it could have had no place in the mind of the first Christians. It is only the importance of the fact, and the facility with which modern ideas are transferred to an ancient context, that make it necessary to state thus plainly, that when the first Christians spoke of the Church existing upon earth, they spoke of an actual and visible society.

Let us now pass to the consideration of the language which is used by our Lord and

His apostles, first of the Church at large, and secondly of its organization and government.

Only twice, so far as we know, did our blessed Lord speak directly of the Church which He intended to found upon earth; once in the memorable promise to St. Peter, that "on this rock will I build my Church," and again when He says of a disciple who has trespassed against his brother, "If he neglect to hear the Church, let him be unto thee as an heathen man and a publican [b]." These passages, even if they stood alone, would go far to indicate to us what our Lord meant by the Church. He meant a visible, tangible society, exercising powers of discipline over its erring members; He meant also a society which was to be founded by and upon an individual apostle, whose great commission, though not different in kind from that of the remaining eleven, was yet first in order, emphatic by its repetition and the peculiar strength of its language, marking thus how strongly, even from its infancy, the stamp of unity was to be impressed upon the Church of Christ.

But these passages do not exhaust what we

[b] [St. Matt. xvi. 18; xviii. 17.]

learn from our Lord as to the nature of His future Church. When He says, for example, that He has "other sheep, which are not of this fold[c]," He foretells, in no uncertain terms, the perfect fusion within her of the Jewish and Gentile elements. When He foretells that the effect of His coming will be not peace, but a sword[d], the severing of the dearest earthly ties, the making to a man foes of the members of his own household,—He intimates, though indirectly, the imperious sovereignty of the union which is to bind Christians to each other. When He bids His apostles make disciples "of all nations, baptizing them in the name of the Father, and of the Son, and of the Holy Ghost;" promising them at the same time that He will be with them "even to the end of the world[e]," He expresses in a few words the universality of the Church, her sacramental character, her Trinitarian faith, and the secret of the eternal duration which He had already promised to her.

But if our Lord speaks but seldom in express terms of His Church, He speaks continually of the kingdom of God and of heaven—expressions

[c] [St. John x. 16.]   [d] [St. Matt. x. 34.]
[e] [St. Matt. xxviii. 19, 20.]

which are evidently not without their bearing on the subject, and which He appears to use in three different but closely allied senses.

Our Lord, then, speaks first of all of the kingdom of God and of heaven as of something future. He commands us to seek for it; to pray for its coming. He connects it with the thought of His own return to judgment. He promises to His apostles places of glory in it. But He speaks of it no less as something actually present, and this either externally or within the heart of men. He likens it, for example, to the leaven which is hid in three measures of meal, diffusing itself by a stealthy and unseen working. He tells His disciples that the kingdom of heaven is within them[f]. While on the other hand He speaks of the mysteries of the kingdom of heaven, of the Word, of the Gospel of the kingdom as something which can now be heard and known; and yet more, He appeals to His command over the evil spirits for a proof that the kingdom of God was actually present, adding the significant words that "something greater than Solomon is here[g]." He likens it, moreover, to the mustard-seed which was to

[f] [St. Luke xvii. 21.] [g] [St. Luke xi. 31 : πλεῖον.]

grow into a goodly plant, to be the refuge and shelter of the nations; it was to be as the fisherman's net, gathering into it good and bad alike. Our Lord, therefore, came to establish upon earth something not unworthy to be called by the name of the Kingdom of God above; something which was at once to have its abode in the hearts of men, and its visible presence in the face of the whole world. The bearing of this teaching upon the idea of the Church is at once obvious and important. While it marks clearly that they are not all Israel who are of Israel[h], and that the external kingdom of heaven here embraces within it bad as well as good, it does identify this kingdom of heaven upon earth with the visible Church of God, and it points no less distinctly to the intimacy of that union which links the Church militant with the Church triumphant above. The doctrine of the Kingdom of the heavens is, in a word, the doctrine of the Communion of Saints. It is also something more. Our Lord planted upon earth not a commonwealth, but a kingdom; and that kingdom was to be the earthly counterpart of one above, in which angels and

[h] [Rom. ix. 6.]

archangels, cherubim and seraphim, principalities and powers, surround the throne of God.

From the words of our Lord we pass to those of the apostles. In the first place, the union between the Church at large and her Lord is brought out with a distinctness which is due to the finished Sacrifice of Christ. The repeated declaration that the Church is the body of Christ is further illustrated by the words in which St. Paul compares the union of Christ and His Church to the marriage-union by which two become one flesh[i], and yet more clearly by the Apocalyptic vision in which the Church is seen arrayed as the Bride of the Lamb[k]. Interpreted in the light of these words, we may see how much more our Lord must have meant by the parable of the Royal Marriage than could have been understood at the time by any who heard it. We may see also how the Church can be the πλήρωμα—the completion of Him who yet filleth all in all[l]; and how the whole dispensation is one long preparation of a glorious Church without spot or wrinkle, to crown the glory of her Lord. So absolute is

---

[i] [1 Cor. xii. 12, 27; Eph. i. 23; v. 25–32.]
[k] [Rev. xxi. 2.]   [l] [Eph. i. 23.]

the unity expressed, that in it is merged in a manner the personal union between Christ and the Christian. He is a member of the one body, a living stone of the one building, which is built upon the foundation of the apostles and prophets, Jesus Christ Himself being the chief Corner-stone[m]. He cannot think in the apostle's words of his union with Christ, without being reminded at the same time that he is a member of the Church.

But this is not all. The spiritual building is built upon the foundation of the apostles and prophets. In this is implied, first, an intimate relation between the present and the older covenants (of which more hereafter), and secondly, that it is built upon the foundation of the apostles, who are presented to us as working together, with an unity of purpose at least not less complete than that of the prophets under the former dispensation. Further[n], we learn in what the unity of the apostolic purpose consisted, when we are told of the Church as being not only the abode of

[m] [Eph. ii. 20, 21.]
[n] [In pencil on margin of MS.: "Re-write—scantily sketched out."]

God, but the "pillar and ground of the truth°." The unity of the truth, and of the Church in which it dwells, implies in its Founder an essential unity of purpose.

Lastly, if the Church be one, it is no less universal. The one baptism into Christ was to efface all distinctions and to unite every race ᴾ.

Then, to sum up, we arrive at the four cardinal notes of the One, Holy, Catholic, and Apostolic Church. We have seen, moreover, and it is essential to observe, that however much some of these notes are expounded and defined in the apostolic writings, the groundwork of all is laid in the words of our Lord Himself. The full import of those words was, indeed, but slowly revealed and imperfectly understood in the first years of the Church: but still there they were: and in the unchanged teaching of the Lord is contained the germ of all which the apostles afterwards proclaimed. The grand outline is drawn by the hand of the Divine Master: it is the work of the disciple to give fuller expression to His meaning.

It remains now to be considered how this character of the Church was in fact to be

° [1 Tim. iii. 15.]   ᴾ Gal. iii. 27, 28; 1 Cor. xii. 13.

maintained; and especially how the primary note of unity was to be prevented from being deformed and lost[q].

How such a Church as this, at once One and Universal, ever became a reality, is the wonder of the world's history. The very idea bore the impress of more than human originality. All previous religions were opposed to it; all previous aspirations after unity (if aspirations they can be called) had been shattered at the moment of their contact with the sober realities of life. No philosophy, however lofty, but dispersed into schools in the hands of its first disciples; no theosophy, however ethereal, but engendered in the minds of its votaries the restlessness of an ungoverned fancy. Sects, mysteries, philosophies, rose, sparkled, and burst, like bubbles upon the stream of time. Nothing attained to permanence which was not rooted in the firm soil of nationality. Christianity, when it declared itself universal, defied the whole experience of mankind; and, historically speaking, the great marvel of Christianity is that

---

[q] [This paragraph was to have been amplified, and "the contents of Acts ii. 42 to be worked in, so far as they are not used already."]

it succeeded in providing an adequate groundwork for this universal cohesion.

The apostles therefore, in fact, express the one doctrine of their Lord,—developed indeed by circumstances, adapted to new wants, exhibiting new aspects, but still essentially one. And in estimating the possibility of this essential unity, it must ever be borne in mind that their teaching rested not simply upon the words of a Master, which would inevitably convey very different impressions to the individual minds who received them, but upon actions and facts of a superhuman character. The apostles were not only teachers; they were, before all things, witnesses.

It is in the light of these facts alone that we can understand the relations which existed between the individual members of the apostolic college. To those who ranged themselves under the names of Paul or Apollos or Cephas[r],—as if they had been the teachers of independent systems, or disciples who had variously modified the system of their great Master,—the answer of the apostle is simple: "Was Paul crucified for you? or were ye baptized in the name of

[r] [1 Cor. i. 12.]

Paul?" Christianity, in other words, is not a matter of doctrine, excepting so far as doctrine leads on to something higher—to the sacramental participation in the atoning sacrifice of Christ.

Yet this fundamental unity does not exclude the variety of individual character, nor make the apostles exceptions to the principle which St. Paul himself lays down, that there are diversities of gifts, though there is but one Holy Spirit[s]. In each apostle, no less than in each humbler disciple, the working of the Spirit expanded, instead of effacing the individuality[t].

[s] [1 Cor. xii. 4.]
[t] [Here was to have followed an analysis of the theology of the several chief apostles.]

CHAPTER VI.[a]

The Government of the Apostolic Church.

HAVING seen, then, from the words of our Lord that He proposed to establish an actual, tangible society, which He called the Church; and having seen further what were the distinctive notes of the Church as unfolded in the teaching, first of the Lord and then of His apostles, we proceed to enquire how much is ascertainable as to the government of the Church in the lifetime of the apostles.

The original commission of the Lord vested the government of the Church entirely in the hands of the Apostles. Although in His lifetime He sent out "other seventy," and imparted to them supernatural powers, His only command to them was to go before His face, into every place where He Himself should

[a] [On margin of MS.: "The connexion with what precedes to be worked up."]

come. With this preparatory work their ministry began and ended. They are nowhere associated with the Twelve, nor is any authority, even of a subordinate kind, committed to them, nor are they even mentioned after their original task was done.

In the first infancy, therefore, the Apostolate included, as in the germ, the whole ministry of the Church. The first delegation of their functions was to the Seven, whose election is related in the sixth chapter of the Acts. The whole form of the narrative, the minuteness of detail, the care with which the names are recorded, all point to the importance which is attached by the inspired historian to the event.

The name of Deacons, by which we usually speak of the Seven, is first given to them, so far as we know, in the second century, by Irenæus[b]; and it may reasonably admit of a question whether their office was really identical with the permanent diaconate of the Church. The identity of the two offices was in fact denied by St. Chrysostom[c], and by a decree of the

[b] [Iren. i. 26, ed. Massuet, vol. i. p. 105.]
[c] [See Chrys. in Act. Ap. Hom. xiv. 3.]

Council in Trullo[d]; in later times by Vitringa, to whose theory the denial was essential; and in more modern times by several writers of distinction. It has been, on the other hand, affirmed by the general voice of tradition. It is urged in confirmation of the more received opinion that the name, though not given by St. Luke to the Seven, is strikingly suggested by his narrative.

The occasion of their election is said to be the complaint which arose of unfairness in the daily διακονία, or administering of the alms of the Church. We have here, then, the word διακονία used for the first time in immediate connexion with the Seven in its distinctively Christian sense of the distribution of alms,— in this special sense of the word, that is, which gave the name to the diaconate. No distinction, moreover, has ever been shewn to exist between the office of the Seven and that of the later deacon. The basis of both is the distribution of alms, and to both alike spiritual duties seem to have been superadded.

If St. Luke does not call them deacons, this is easily explained by the unfixed use of titles,

[d] [Can. 16, quoted by Bingham, Bk. II. Ch. xx. § 1.]

of which we shall see presently yet larger and more surprising instances. But it certainly is remarkable that after having mentioned with studious and emphatic care the election of the Seven, he says nothing whatever of the first appointment of Presbyters, but mentions them incidentally[e] for the first time as exercising, at Jerusalem itself, the very office to which the Seven were appointed.

Throughout the Acts of the Apostles we meet with no distinct evidence of the existence of any but a single order of ministers subordinate to the apostles. When St. Paul is founding the Churches of Asia Minor, he everywhere ordains them presbyters[f]; at the Council of Jerusalem presbyters alone are mentioned as distinct from the body of the brethren[g]; and the only cases in which persons are found in the discharge of functions which suggest the later service of the deacon are those of Mark and Timothy, whose importance makes it little probable that they held an office inferior to that of the general body of the presbyters.

[e] [Acts xi. 30.]   [f] [Acts xiv. 23.]
[g] [Acts xv. 4, &c.]

The natural inference would appear to be that the Seven are indeed the original deacons of the Church; but that they are also something more. So long as the Church was almost confined to Jerusalem, it is probable that the distinctive duties of a presbyter were still discharged by the apostles. But the enlargement of the Church entailed, as an immediate consequence, an enlargement of the functions of the inferior minister. The Seven, increased in number and invested with higher powers, would become the original presbyters, as they had been the original deacons; there being, however, as yet but a single order, in which the double functions of presbyter and deacon were united.

But the process of expansion which had led first to the creation of the Seven and then to the enlargement of their office, was still going forward; the personal government of the Church by the hands of the apostles was becoming daily less and less continuous; and in the Epistle to the Philippians[h] we find for the first time an explicit mention of the two orders of "the bishops and deacons."

[h] [Phil. i. 1.]

As soon, however, as we come to a mention of a plurality of orders, we are met by some difficulty arising from the uncertain use of terms. In the Christian ministry it has happened, as often elsewhere in history, that the thing has preceded the name. The very name of Apostle is used in the New Testament with an uncertainty which has led to serious question. The name of Bishop, when it first appears, is so used as to imply that it was then not a term of office at all; while in the later writings of the Canon, it is found sometimes as entirely synonymous with πρεσβύτερος, sometimes as suggesting the idea that the title of Presbyter or Elder was preferred by the Jewish Christians familiar with the service of the synagogue, the title of Bishop or Overseer by the Churches of Gentile origin, to whom doubtless it would sound strange to call a young man by the venerable title of Elder. Other names are used for the ministers of either order. The Deacon appears in the Pastoral Epistles to be described as νεώτερος, or Younger; the Presbyters are spoken of as Leaders (ἡγούμενοι) and Presidents (προϊστάμενοι); St. Mark, again, is called the Servant or Minister (ὑπηρέτης) of SS. Paul and

Barnabas; and in one passage we find collective mention of the Presbytery[i].

Yet with all this diversity of expression it appears clearly enough that at some time preceding the Roman imprisonment of St. Paul, it had been found necessary to relieve the presbyters of a part of their inferior duties,—just as in the infancy of the Church the apostles had themselves been relieved,—and to constitute a separate order of deacons.

But the time was fast approaching when other provision would be necessary for the due government of the Church. Hitherto the apostles, though relieved of that constant charge which would have fixed them to a single spot, still had upon their hands the "care of all the Churches[k]." Their ordination, their discipline, their divisions, their scandals, their advances, all passed beneath the vigilant eye of the apostles, who were thus, in our sense of the word, the bishops of the whole Church. But this could not last. As the reins of power fell from the hands of the apostles, they would

---

[i] [See 1 Tim. v. 1; Tit. ii. 6; Heb. xiii. 17; 1 Thess. v. 12; cf. 1 Tim. v. 12; Acts xiii. 5; 1 Tim. iv. 14.]

[k] [2 Cor. xi. 28.]

of necessity pass into some other hands; and as it became clear that it was not the will of God that the career of the Church should close with the life of the apostles, it was necessary for those who had themselves guided her from the first day of Pentecost, as the immediate delegates of Christ, to decide, under God, the final and most momentous question of the manner of her future government: whether, in other words, their office was wholly to die with themselves, or whether, on the other hand, they were to leave successors to that part of their bishopric which could alone by the nature of the case be perpetuated.

Yet the very gradual way in which the apostles were withdrawn, partly by death and partly by other circumstances, from the personal control of the Church, would lead us to expect that any appointment of successors, if resolved upon by the apostles, would only be gradually made.

And in point of fact we find that the office of a bishop, in his two distinctive functions of individual government of a Church and of the power of ordaining others, is found to exist in certain exceptional cases before the death of St. Paul: it is found to be universal before the death of St. John. The first instance, indeed, in which one who was not a member of the Twelve had been placed in sole charge of a Church had occurred comparatively early, and included in itself the principle of all that was to follow.

Before the dispersion of the Twelve in the great persecution of Herod, they committed the charge of the mother Church of Jerusalem to James the brother of the Lord. We shall not err if we follow the voice of all early tradition when we consider him to have been not one of the Twelve, but to have been, in the true sense of the word, the first Christian bishop.

It is to St. James, as the head of the Church of Jerusalem, that St. Peter addresses his parting message when, after his miraculous escape, he retires from the Holy City. It is St. James who presides in the first Christian Council—an important acknowledgment of the principle of local authority. It is St. James who, with all the presbyters, receives St. Paul upon his return from Greece. It is St. James, lastly, who in the Epistle to the Galatians occupies that first place which is elsewhere assigned to St. Peter;

not assuredly from any wish on the part of St. Paul to depreciate the due position of St. Peter, but because he is writing of Jerusalem and of the acts of the local Council[1].

He thus appears to have occupied within the Church of Jerusalem a position in some respects higher than that of the apostles themselves, and it is only what we should expect from the narrative of the New Testament when we find him recognised by the concordant voice of tradition as the first Bishop of Jerusalem.

Yet his position was, in important respects, exceptional. The veneration accorded to the peculiar holiness of his life, and to his near connexion with the Lord, could as little be transferred to another man as the most sacred associations and metropolitan authority of Jerusalem could be transplanted to another city. And therefore for years he remained as the only Christian bishop.

If we pass by the precarious reference to an anonymous bishop at Philippi, and to Archippus as Bishop of Colosse [m], the earliest canonical mention of such an officer beyond the precincts

[1] [Acts xii. 17; xv. 13; xxi. 18; Gal. ii. 9.]
[m] [Phil. ii. 25; Col. iv. 17.]

of Jerusalem is to be found in the Pastoral Epistles of St. Paul. The charge committed by him to Timothy and to Titus includes not only the general government of a Church by a single individual, but the power of ordaining both presbyters and deacons. They were not only to be conspicuous as teachers and examples of the flock, but to govern even the elders, to regulate their duties and honour, to receive accusations against them, to control the selection of widows to fill the office of deaconess, to admonish, and if need be, to excommunicate the heretical [n]. The most sacred office of ordaining others to the ministry is the subject of special and minute injunctions [o]. Up to this time we have no trace of ordination by any who are not apostles; though even then, as ever since in the Church, the presbyters joined in the laying on of hands [p]. So Timothy had himself been ordained; so doubtless he was in turn to ordain others. And this consenting act of the presbyters expresses something as

[n] [1 Tim. i. 3, 17; v. 9, 17, 19, 20; 2 Tim. iv. 2; Tit. i. 11; ii. 15; iii. 10.]
[o] [1 Tim. iii. 1–13; v. 22; Tit. i. 5.]
[p] [1 Tim. iv. 14.]

to the manner in which men were chosen for the office. In the appointment of the Seven the whole body of believers selected, the apostles ratified and ordained q; but the circumstances of that election were in every way peculiar, and the nature of the complaints which were current was in itself a reason against the selection of the Seven by the apostles. It is a precedent, therefore, on which no heavy stress can be laid. From the proceedings of St. Paul and from his Pastoral Epistles, we learn with certainty thus much, that with the apostle or the bishop it lay to decide absolutely whether the candidate was indeed duly qualified. There is no word of an advising council, no hint of consulting the presbytery—at their own responsibility they gave or they withheld the laying on of their hands. It is not quite so clear by whom the candidates were at first selected. The language of St. Paul to Titus certainly suggests the idea that it lay with him. But the Church of Crete was young, and far from completely organized; and in writing to Timothy in the more ordered Church of Ephesus, he uses no language from which

q [Acts vi. 3-6.]

an inference on this head is possible. Sometimes we know that, as in the case of St. Paul and Timothy themselves, the Holy Spirit intimated through the medium of prophecy the choice to be made of a minister. Always we may presume from the very form of ordination that the consent of the presbyters was necessary. Beyond this we know really nothing, except that the whole tenor of apostolic conduct is evidence that no minister would be forced upon a reluctant Church.

That the office committed to Timothy and to Titus was in fact episcopal in the full range of its power, is beyond a serious question. It has, however, been contended that their commission differed essentially from that of the proper bishop, in being only temporary. To Timothy it is intimated in the first Epistle [r] that the only need for the apostolic instructions depends on the chance of the apostle's delayed return. In the second he is bidden to come to the apostle himself, leaving the Church of Ephesus [s]. And Titus in the same way is bidden, after setting in order the things which are wanting in Crete, to join the apostle at Nicopolis [t].

[r] [1 Tim. i. 3.]   [s] [2 Tim. iv. 9, 21.]   [t] [Tit. iii. 12.]

The objection in the case of Titus admits only of the answer that the injunction of St. Paul is utterly insufficient to support the conclusion which has thus been based upon it. The assumption, therefore, that the commission of Titus was temporary, is one of pure conjecture, and without a known parallel in the whole history of the Church. In the case of Timothy the reply is yet more complete; for the apostle bases the peculiar earnestness of his language upon the assurance which he possesses that the time of his own departure was at hand, and that Timothy would have to meet, without the aid of the apostle, the perils of a time when men would not endure sound doctrine, or the discipline of an ordered ministry [u]. The work of Timothy, therefore, was not to end with his winter's visit to St. Paul; it was to be renewed with even greater earnestness when St. Paul was removed by death.

But if we cannot admit the existence of a reasonable doubt that the office of Timothy and Titus was in the fullest sense episcopal, it may be freely granted that we have no reason to suppose that every Christian Church was as

[u] [2 Tim. iv. 1-6.]

yet governed by a bishop. But before the close of the century the exception had plainly become the rule. The seven Churches of the Apocalypse have each of them its angel [x], of whom Christ speaks as the seven stars in His right hand, to whom the apostle is bidden to address the letters for the Churches, and one of whom is rebuked for the weakness with which he suffers the impure life and unhallowed teaching of his wife [y].

The angel is, therefore, the person charged with the government of the Church, and its chosen representative in the presence of Christ Himself [z].

As we pass beyond the sacred pages of the Canon, the evidence upon the subject divides itself into two classes. We have—

1. The statements of early writers to what was actually existing in the Church of their own day;

2. The statements of later writers as to what was held in their time to be the origin of the Episcopal order.

---

[x] Döllinger [First Age of the Church, E. T., ii.] 120.
[y] [Rev. ii. 20.]
[z] [A reference in MS. to Malachi.]

We will examine each in turn.

1. The earliest Christian writing which has descended to us beyond the pale of Scripture is the Epistle of Clement to the Corinthians. It cannot be assigned to a later date than the year 97; it has even been thought by some to have been written in A.D. 65. It would not, therefore, be quite inconsistent with the apostolic origin of episcopacy, if we found that in the Church of Corinth there was as yet no bishop. And it has not escaped the observation of presbyterian critics, that no bishop is mentioned; that the Corinthians are more than once enjoined to obey, not their bishops, but their presbyters. It is of course possible that this might be occasioned by the letter being written at the instance of the bishop himself; it is also possible that the differences which the letter was written to repress had broken out on occasion of their bishop's death. In determining whether one of these two explanations is to be taken, or whether, on the other hand, the Corinthian Church was not as yet subjected to episcopal government, we turn naturally to see what guidance is afforded by the remaining contents of the Epistle.

The continuity of the Church under the old and new covenants is the leading thought of Clement. It is even more prominent in his Epistle than it is in the Epistle of St. James. Abraham is our father; Christians are the true Israel; theirs are the promises and the blessings of either covenant. Therefore when correcting the disorders which had crept into the divine service, he says [a]; "We ought to do all things in order, which the Lord commanded us to perform in their appointed seasons.... Those then who make their oblations at the appointed seasons are acceptable to God and blessed; for they who follow the injunctions of the Lord do not err. For to the High Priest his own liturgies are given, and to the Priests their own place is allotted, and on the Levites their own ministries are laid. The layman is bound by the lay precepts. Let each of you, brethren, in his own order give thanks (εὐχαριστείτω) to God, walking reverently in a good conscience, and not overstepping the appointed limit of his service (λειτουργίας)[b]."

These certainly are strange expressions for a writer who was not cognizant of three orders

[a] [c. 40.]   [b] [Ibid.]

in the ministry of the Christian Church. But he goes on to blame the Corinthians for arbitrarily deposing presbyters from their office. He says [c]: "Our apostles knew from our Lord Jesus Christ that there would be contention about the dignity of the episcopate; and therefore, being endowed with perfect foresight, they ordained such men, and afterwards gave command (ἐπινομήν) that, when they should be deceased, other approved men should succeed to their office. Those, then, who were constituted either by them, or afterwards by other selected (ἐλλογίμων) men, with the approval of the whole Church ... may not lawfully be deposed."

In this passage by the episcopate is meant simply the priestly office. Clement, indeed, speaks everywhere of "bishops and deacons" as including the whole clergy, and knows nothing of a separate and fixed title of office for him whom we call the bishop. His usage in this respect is exactly that of St. Paul, and shews conclusively that the office has not long been established. More than this, we have already seen, it cannot be held to prove. If we would learn the real meaning of Clement, we must

[c] [c. 44.]

look not to the use of a yet unformed phraseology, but to that which is involved in his actual statements of fact. Whatever be the office to which the apostles commanded that successors should be provided, whether that of the presbyters or that of the apostles themselves, the statement of Clement is explicit, that the apostles acted on the immediate command of Christ, to perpetuate the ministry of the Church. But he says more. He says that the presbyters had been, in fact, constituted either by the apostles themselves, or afterwards "by other selected men." To these men, therefore, who are thus placed immediately below the apostles, and to them alone, was committed the charge of ordaining others. Can any fair mind doubt that we have here a description of such as Timothy and Titus?

Passing by the very questionable Epistles of Barnabas and Hermas, we are next met by the celebrated Epistles of Ignatius.

Without entering here upon the defence of the genuineness of the Seven Epistles, it may be well at least to bear in mind that this celebrated controversy is now reduced within very narrow limits. It is now practically admitted that the Epistles, even if forged, must have seen the light before the year 140. It is also admitted with an unanimity scarcely less complete, that the theory of Mr. Cureton, by which the stamp of genuineness was confined to the wreck of three Epistles, fails upon closer scrutiny, and that the writer of the three, be he who he may, is also the writer of the seven. Who that writer was, I shall not affect to doubt. Ignatius, Bishop of Antioch, a disciple of the apostle John, while falling far short of his great master in his largeness of heart and in his heavenly depth of character, yet makes us feel, by two remarkable traits, the truth of his relation to the beloved apostle. The leading thought of his theology might fitly be expressed in the very words of St. John, " He that believeth not that Jesus Christ is come in the flesh, the same is a deceiver and an antichrist [d]." Round the true Incarnation of God is centred to him the whole mystery of the faith. The leading idea of his active life as bishop was evidently that which is also impressed upon all that we know of the later life of St. John, that in his day the great need

[d] [See 2 John 7.]

of the Church was a more compact discipline, and a more present sense of unity [e]. Living at the moment when the last of the apostles had just been withdrawn from the Church, he felt how entirely the maintenance of this unity depended upon the episcopal office. He felt this all the more deeply because his home was in one of the intellectual capitals of Gnosticism, with its acute, restless criticism, its eclectic, intensely disintegrating spirit. Therefore to him the primary importance of episcopacy is, that in it the Church is one. He speaks in one breath of men being severed "from their God Jesus Christ, from their bishop, and from the precepts of the apostles." He tells the presbyters that they are united to their bishop as chords to the lyre. He even congratulates them on being united to their bishop as the Church is to Christ, and as Christ to the Father. Every bishop, he assures them, is the vicar of Christ. As Christ stood to the apostles, so the bishop stands to the presbyters. Without the three orders, he says again, of bishop, priest, and deacon, no Church exists. The bishop's authority is necessary to the valid

[e] Ad Philad. c. 8, Rothe, p. 479.

administration of the Sacraments; his sanction should be had for every marriage union [f].

Language like this, written on the very morrow of the apostolic age, by a man who had himself been consecrated by apostolic hands, venerated as a saint in his life, as a martyr in his death, speaks almost for itself. It is indeed the language only of an individual bishop, and of one doubtless of somewhat peculiar temperament, and placed under somewhat peculiar circumstances. It is, at the very least, an honest testimony to the fact that in the day immediately succeeding the apostles, episcopacy was universal in the Church of Christ, and was believed, at least by one who had himself been honoured with high apostolic confidence, to be, by God's ordinance, essential to the very being of Church and Sacraments.

But the language of St. Ignatius is observable not only for what it expresses, but also for that of which it implies the absence. It has been thought by some that the existence of metropolitan authority is recognisable even in the New Testament itself. It is remarkable that the Bishop of Antioch appears to know nothing

[f] [Ad Trall. 7; Eph. 4, 5; Magn. 6; Trall. 3; Smyrn. 8; Polyc. 5.]

of it. Every bishop is to him alike the vicar of Christ, and the very strength of the images which he uses to express his sacred authority seem almost to preclude the idea of anything higher. And yet this is not for want of extending his view beyond the Churches to which he is actually writing. He says, for example, that "Jesus Christ, our inseparable life, is the mind of the Father, as also the bishops, who are constituted throughout the world, are in the mind of Jesus Christ." And again, "Where the bishop is, there let the multitude be; even as where Jesus Christ is, there is the Catholic Church g." In these passages he shews that the thought of the Catholic Church was clearly present to his mind. It would certainly seem also that he held the mind of the Church to be expressed in the deciding voice of her bishops. And yet the only mention or hint of any communication between Church and Church is to be found in the advice given to the Churches of Philadelphia and Smyrna, that they should send a deacon to Antioch and the neighbouring Churches to congratulate them upon the close of their persecution h.

g [Ad Eph. 3; Smyrn. 8.]   h [Ad Philad. 10; Smyrn. 11.]

It is, of course, quite true that we cannot infer with certainty from the language of St. Ignatius that metropolitan authority did not as yet exist; but it is assuredly clear that, if existing, it was as yet weak and insignificant. Nor is this the only point which shews that episcopacy was yet in its infancy when these Epistles were written. The language of later writers with regard to the prerogative of the bishop is guarded by the anxious thought that the glorious ideal might be marred, and the bishop himself be untrue even to the foundation of the faith. Such a thought has evidently never crossed the mind of Ignatius. He rests in the following of the bishop as a safe and certain guide. The Church, therefore, when he wrote, can as yet have had no experience of deep unfaithfulness in the highest office of her ministry; nothing which could shake her trust in the guidance of her chief pastors.

If anything that is peculiar in the temperament and circumstances of St. Ignatius should seem in any measure to detract from the great weight of his witness, the same rule must add double value to the testimony of Irenæus—a man whose judicial fairness and rare catholicity, of spirit were outshone only by his deep love of peace. And his language is unquestionably far more measured than that of the fervid Bishop of Antioch. Yet the substance of his teaching on the subject of episcopacy differs only from that of Ignatius as we should expect from the interval of half a century which had elapsed between them.

In opposition to the pretensions of the Gnostic teachers he writes [i]: "True knowledge is the doctrine of the apostles, and the ancient system of the Church throughout the world, and the mark of the body of Christ according to the succession of the bishops to whom they (the apostles) committed the several Churches." And he speaks repeatedly of the guarantee afforded by this episcopal succession for the identity of the existing doctrine of the Church with that of the apostles themselves [k]. Thus far he and Ignatius utter the same language. It is instructive, however, to observe the respects in which they differ from each other. While Ignatius urges his readers to cling to their individual bishop, safe in the guidance

[i] [Iren. iv. 33, ed. Massuet, vol. i. p. 272.]
[k] [See Iren. iii. 2, 3; iv. 26, ed. Massuet, vol. i. pp. 175, 262.]

of the holder of such an office, Irenæus looks rather to the security which the succession as a whole affords; he looks, in short, more to the office, and less to the individual bishop; more to the Catholic world, and less to the individual Church.

We see in him, moreover, an unmistakeable indication that the want of a centre for Christendom had been felt, and was beginning to be supplied by the primacy of the Church of Rome. He gives the succession of her bishops as the obvious type and example of all similar successions, adding as his reason, that "to this Church, on account of its pre-eminence, every Church must come[1],"—words indeed of very indefinite meaning, but which become important in the light of later history. He holds, indeed, more clearly even than Ignatius, that it is the general consent of the Churches which is the pledge of the purity of the Christian faith; but he holds also, that Rome, on account of its pre-eminence among apostolic Churches, as the seat of empire, as the tomb of the two great apostles whom it claimed as its joint founders, and lastly, no doubt, as the largest and most influential

[1] [Iren. iii. 3.]

body of Christians in the world, is in a manner the *ecclesia prærogativa*, the mouthpiece through which the one voice of the Church would be most legitimately uttered. Of this, Ignatius, though writing to the Romans, shews himself entirely unconscious; and, in fact, the circumstances out of which it arose were precisely the growth of the half century which intervened between our two writers. When Ignatius wrote, the government of all the Churches had very lately fallen from the apostolic hands of St. John. Ephesus then was still radiant with his memory. Antioch and Corinth both shared with Rome the honour of a foundation by the joint labours of SS. Peter and Paul; Jerusalem, which had risen again from her ashes, was still regarded by all Jewish Christians as the mother of all the Churches, and was invested in the eyes of every Christian with associations too sacred to allow of her being readily postponed to any other Church. In the fifty years which followed, the revolt of Barcochab had finally removed Jerusalem; the fresh glory of St. John had faded away from Ephesus; and as the need of a Christian metropolis made itself increasingly felt, the prestige of Rome told decisively in its favour, and the capital of the Empire became the capital of the Church.

It is needless to carry further this branch of our evidence.

2. We turn to examine the evidence of post-apostolic writers as to what was held in their time to be the origin of the episcopal order.

Of this evidence something has been anticipated in what has just been said. The value of the rest, though slight compared with what we have seen, to establish the fact that episcopacy was indeed founded by the apostles, is not small to those who have admitted the fact, as the source of some further light upon the time and mode of its foundation.

First, then, there is a certain amount of evidence which points to St. John as the chief, though not the exclusive organizer of the episcopal order.

We have, first of all, the express assertion of Tertullian that "the order of bishops if traced back to its origin will rest upon John as its author [m]." By these words it is evident that he did not mean to speak of St. John as the

[m] [Adv. Marc. iv. 5.]

only apostle who had planted episcopal Churches; for he speaks himself elsewhere of the consecration of Clement of Rome by St. Peter [n]. He means, rather,* that episcopacy as an universal order was diffused by St. John; and Clement of Alexandria partly confirms his words. While relating a celebrated anecdote, for the truth of which he vouches with special emphasis, he says that St. John, after the death of Domitian, left Patmos and returned to Ephesus, and that thence he was wont to travel into the neighbouring countries, "here to place bishops, there to organize whole Churches [o]." It is, moreover, in complete accordance with the little we otherwise know of the active ministry of St. John. If Ignatius could truly speak of himself as a man "prepared for the work of union [p]," he might have said it in a far higher sense of the last and greatest of the apostles. It is not alone in his theology, where he seems to blend all paler rays of truth in the blaze of a heavenly light, it is also in his government of the Church that we feel the peculiar gift of St. John [q].

[n] [De Præscr. Hær. 32.] [o] [Clem. apud Eus. iii. 23.]
[p] [Ad Philad. 8.]   [q] Thiersch [Ap. Age], p. 274, &c.

His fixing the observance of Easter in harmony with the Paschal associations of the Jews, his care to maintain the terms of the compact by which their feelings had been consulted in the Council of Jerusalem, and again to exhibit, by wearing the priestly πέταλον [r], how the sacrifice of the older covenant was continued under the new in a mystic and spiritual form; all these things shew a peculiar and most loving desire to blend in the most perfect unity the Jewish and the Gentile converts. But if he was thus willing to bring out into the strongest possible relief those points which were calculated to draw Christians together, he was severe beyond example in his reprobation of those who resisted these loving efforts, and after all had been done to win them, persisted in heresy and division. The well-known story of his flying from the baths which contained the heretic Cerinthus [s], is in perfect harmony with the stern language of the third Epistle of St. John, and of the rebukes contained in the letters to the seven angels. The disciple of love is still the Son of Thunder; and the gentlest of all spirits towards those who are within the fold, is compatible

[r] [Polycrates ap. Eus. iii. 31.]   [s] [See Eus. iii. 28.]

with an inflexible severity in guarding its defences from the encroachments of the stranger and the robber.

This same conclusion, again, that St. John was the great organizer of episcopacy, would be suggested, even apart from this evidence, by a careful comparison of the opening chapters of the Apocalypse with the Pastoral Epistles on the one hand, and those of St. Ignatius on the other. The immense chasm which divides the rudimentary order of the Churches planted by St. Paul from the rigorously defined and universal episcopacy which we find described by Ignatius, might well seem too wide to be bridged by half a century. There is nothing like it in history. The more we look into the circumstances, the more the marvel grows. A form of government, entirely original in itself, and of which some thirty years after the ascension of our blessed Lord the Church exhibits only a few exceptional instances, is in fifty years afterwards accepted by the whole Christian world, and freely spoken of by the foremost Christians of the day as a matter of Divine institution. And this in a society composed of Jews and Gentiles, whose opposing views and sympathies had taxed the highest energies of apostles to keep them at all within the pale of the common Church.

By what possible agency, we might well ask, could such a change have been wrought: what iron will had bent to an unanimity so difficult and so perfect the scattered Church of Christ? The seven Churches of Asia are the key to the mysterious problem, and point, with Tertullian, to St. John as the true founder of episcopacy.

But this reply suggests two other and yet more difficult questions. Can it be that St. John in so momentous a change acted without all human counsel? Can we know anything at all more precisely of the circumstances under which the change was introduced?

In answer to the first it must be borne in mind that prior to any general establishment of episcopal order in the Church, bishops had been fixed in certain important cities. The cases of St. James, of Timothy, and of Titus, have already been before us. We have traditional evidence that the like step had been taken in some other Churches. Of the infancy of the Church of Rome, owing to the significant silence of Scripture, we have received accounts so conflicting that it is impossible to speak without a certain hesitation. But that there was a bishop there before the martyrdom of the apostles Peter and Paul, there seems no reason to doubt. It is most probable that the first bishop, Linus, was consecrated immediately before their martyrdom, and by their joint authority. At Antioch, too, and at Alexandria, traditions of less value ascribe to St. Peter and St. Paul [t] the consecration of bishops; so that this at least is clear, that before the taking of Jerusalem approaches had been made to an episcopal government of the Church, and some preparation made for the organization of the whole Church by St. John. But yet it would certainly be in accordance with what we know of apostolic action that St. John in such a matter should have acted with such counsel as was accessible to him; and we naturally enquire therefore whether there is any trace of a meeting of the surviving apostles subsequent to the martyrdom of the two apostles at Rome.

Now there are, in fact, two passages from early Church writers, the one expressly stating,

[t] [Sic in orig.]

the other seeming to imply, the fact of some such meeting. The first is from Eusebius [u], who says: "There is a tradition that after the martyrdom of James and the taking of Jerusalem, which follows immediately upon it, those of the apostles and of the disciples of the Lord who were yet living came together from all parts, together with those who were of the kindred of the Lord according to the flesh," to elect a successor to St. James. The exact amount of authority to be assigned to this tradition we have no means of ascertaining; but there is some reason to believe it to be derived from the narrative of Hegesippus [x]. In connection with this is to be taken a remarkable fragment of Irenæus, in which he says that "those who have followed the second ordinances of the apostles know that the Lord has ordained a new Offering in the New Covenant, according to the prophet Malachi [y]." The most obvious interpretation of these words is that the apostles held a Council, which is here compared as second with that recorded in the Acts [z]. Nor can it

---

[u] [Hist. Eccl.] iii. 11.   [x] Rothe 354, 60.
[y] [Iren. Fragm. 2, ed. Massuet, vol. ii. p. 10.]
[z] For other interpretations, see Harvey, Iren. ii. 500.

fairly be urged against this sense of the passage that the authority of these second ordinances is said to be only partially admitted. As much might have been said in the time even of Irenæus of the first decrees of Jerusalem. And it is well worthy of note that if we accept the statement of Eusebius as true, and believe that an apostolic Council was held soon after the taking of Jerusalem, it is impossible not to suppose that so precious an opportunity would have been employed for the settlement of other questions affecting the dearest interests of the Church. But if so, the question which Irenæus asserts the apostles to have decided is precisely one which at that hour would have called for the clearest expression of apostolical judgment. The Temple had been destroyed; the sacrifices upon which the Hebrew Christians had ever diligently waited, had now come to an end. What course were they to take? what substitute, if any, were they to find in the ordinances of the Second Covenant? To them therefore, at such a moment, an assurance from the whole apostolic body that in the Eucharist they would find a fulfilment of all their needs must have been an especial comfort. True it is, no doubt, that the doctrine itself cannot have been new or strange to them. The Epistle to the Hebrews, which is so impregnated with it, was already in the hands of many of them; and there is some reason to believe that St. James had laid especial stress upon it. It is yet easy to perceive that an explicit declaration upon this great doctrine would have emanated, almost of course, from an apostolical Council held at such a juncture. But if so, there exists between the two statements of Eusebius and Irenæus a complete and remarkable harmony. Eusebius suggests the occasion to which the words of Irenæus refer; Irenæus removes the apparent strangeness of a Council, assembled with so much effort, for the election of a single bishop.

But if we can infer thus much with a high probability of truth, we may be almost morally certain that we have before us the occasion on which the systematic establishment of the episcopal order was decreed. In the election of Simeon the son of Clopas to be bishop of Jerusalem we have, in short, not the choice of a single bishop, but a solemn decision on the part of those to whom Christ had committed His Church that the time had come for them to set her future government upon a firm and lasting basis.

There is therefore reasonable ground for believing that the general diffusion of episcopacy inaugurated the second apostolic age, to which St. John may be said to have given his name. What is certain is, that before his death the great work was accomplished.

It remains to be seen by what duties and privileges the various orders of the Christian ministry were distinguished.

* * * * * *

DOGMATIC PREACHING.

AN ESSAY ON DOGMATIC PREACHING:

Written for the Church Congress of 1866.

THE office of Christian preaching would seem to be not so much to attract and to inform, as to produce a change of heart in those who are indifferent to religion, and to sustain and strengthen in those who are *not* the power of the spiritual life. All communication of knowledge, therefore, from the pulpit, whether it be historical, moral, or doctrinal, is simply a means to a given end. The question before us is, how this end is best to be attained.

It is clear, moreover, that preaching—proposing to itself such an end as this—must appeal to motives of no common order; and that the higher the motives which it can effectually bring to bear upon the heart of man, the greater is the hope of any true success.

Thus much, perhaps, will be admitted on all

hands. The moment, however, we come to consider what are the highest motives which are recognised by the heart of man, we receive, in substance, one of two answers, upon which are based two opposite schools of preaching, which are as contradictory in their whole conception and course as they are in their answer to this fundamental question.

The one school makes its highest appeal to the sense which exists within man of the good, the beautiful, and the true; the other places foremost the prostrate misery of his nature in the presence of the over-mastering power of evil, and the inextinguishable yearning for a help which is above and beyond his own. The one attempts, in short, to raise man by an appeal to his strength, the other by an appeal to his weakness.

The first of these, which appeals to the love of what is good and beautiful and true, holds these motives to have been rectified in man by the influence of the work of Christ, and that being so rectified and elevated through Him, they now form a basis of noble and heavenward aspiration, to which the preacher may safely appeal as a motive, and which has the merit of being as universal as it is noble; for it comes home, in its degree, to every one, whatever his previous teaching or form of belief may have been. Christianity, as so presented, is in short synonymous with moral goodness. It is a Christianity, therefore, of the largest toleration, for it recognises as a part of itself whatever is good and pure and true, not only without distinction of sect or Church, but even beyond the very pale of Christendom. There are, of course, shades of difference which come under this general conception of the office of preaching. For the highest moral goodness one will substitute the harmonious development of humanity; another will appeal to the beautiful more directly than to the true, and set before himself æsthetic beauty as the basis of his religious appeal to the heart; a third will seem almost to identify religion with manliness. But whatever these minor variations, the general theory is the same, that the highest evidence for religion lies in the witness of the heart, and its correspondence with our conceptions of what is noble and good and true,—and, as an inference from this, that the appeal to those conceptions is the most effective mode of preaching it.

But this kind of preaching, or rather the idea of religion which underlies it, and of which it is the natural expression, is open to this fundamental objection. It is entirely one-sided in its estimate of that humanity which it aspires to influence so profoundly. It rests on a denial of the nature and depth of sin; and it implies that the whole result of Christianity upon the present life of man consists in a certain elevation of his moral standard, which is directly traceable to the peerless teaching and the spotless example of our Lord. It amounts therefore to a denial of the gift of a personal and indwelling Spirit, and of the perpetual intercession of Christ. It even goes far to undermine belief in His Divinity and Atoning Sacrifice; for, ignoring as it does our individual need of a Saviour, it leaves no intelligible motive for so stupendous a work. It reduces sacraments to a symbol, and miracle to one vast enigma—one long and unmeaning interference with the course of natural law. If this, we may well say, is the sum of Christianity, then Christ has died in vain. By whatever name it may be called, in whatever communion it may take refuge, such preaching is in principle, and in its certain issue, Socinian.

If it should seem that even this brief mention of such a school of preaching is out of place here, I might answer, I fear, that such preaching is unhappily current, and that it exercises a secret influence upon many who emphatically repudiate its principles. But, in fact, without it I should have found it hard to state, with any clearness, the questions which appear to me to be at issue, among really orthodox Christians, on the subject of dogmatic preaching.

In strong contrast, then, with this school, which is undogmatic in its preaching, because it is anti-dogmatic in its belief, is that which starts, as a first principle, from the sinfulness of man and his consequent need of a Saviour.

The preaching of this school must always be, in a certain sense and to a certain degree, dogmatic. The very mention of a Saviour,—of One who not only taught an unequalled morality and left an unapproachable example, but who Redeemed us, and bought us with the price of His blood,—compels questions as to the nature of His work and of His relation to us which are essentially dogmatic. If we start, for instance, from the point on which St. Paul takes his stand, as essential to Christian preaching, the resurrection of our Lord, and follow it out even in the most meagre way, it will be seen that the fact of the resurrection leads to inquiry as to the power in virtue of which it was possible, and from which it derives its significance. It implies, therefore, almost immediately, as we look backwards, the doctrines of Christ's Sacrifice and Incarnation—and as we look forwards, it can hardly dwell upon the mind without suggesting the Eternal Session at the right hand of the Father, the mission of the Comforter, and the final return to Judgment. If, then, we accept this position, we must admit that Dogma lies at the root of all Christian preaching. But if so, the question of dogmatic preaching is, in fact, narrowed to this:— Whether it is more desirable in the pulpit to express doctrine distinctly, to enlarge on it, illustrate it, appeal to it constantly as a practical motive to action, use it, in short, as the great staple of our preaching;—or, on the other hand, to preach habitually the necessity of that holy life which Christ's coming has alone made possible, without dwelling in detail upon the means through which it has so come to be possible; in other words, to imply doctrine, rather than to express it.

The moment, however, the question is reduced within such limits as these, it becomes to some extent a question of more or less,—of time and place and circumstance,—with which it is very hard to deal in any general form. Whatever, therefore, is said, I must ask you kindly to understand as said with reserve of exceptional cases and positions.

It will enable us, perhaps, to consider better how far an indirect teaching of Christianity is possible, if we set before ourselves a simple picture of what Christianity is. It is a life spent in communion with Christ; we in Him and He in us, He the Head and we the members, one with Him by mystical regeneration, and by Sacramental participation in His atoning Sacrifice. It is a life sustained by the indwelling of the Holy Spirit, who helps our infirmities and who pleads for us with groanings which cannot be uttered. It is a life watched over by Angels, and assisted by the prayers of the Church in earth and heaven. It is a life of conflict against the principalities and the powers of a world of darkness. It is a continual watching against the wiles of the Devil, who is going about, seeking whom he may devour. It is a life, moreover, of hope and of faith; a life whose pilgrimage is here, but whose citizenship is in heaven. It is a life, lastly, of praise and adoration of Him who has created us, of Him who has redeemed us, of Him who sustains us and loves us with an everlasting love. It is a life, in short, in which at every turn the deepest spring of action is a supernatural fact. We preach the necessity of a life which nothing but a supernatural power can maintain, and to which, for the most part, nothing but the hope of heaven and the fear of hell can stimulate the dull and hardened heart. How is it possible, I would ask, to preach such a life, without a continual appeal to the doctrines upon which this life is to be built? How is it possible to preach Christ, without keeping clearly and continually before men who Christ is, what He has done, what He is doing now, what He will do hereafter—or without shewing clearly the nature of the Christian conflict, and of the depth of that corruption which penetrates even to the world of spirits?

But it will be answered, perhaps—You mistake the question at issue. You have used dogma, doctrine, supernatural fact, as if they were synonymous: whereas, what is really objected to, by those who complain of dogmatic preaching, is not the appeal to supernatural facts in preaching, nor even to theological doctrine, as found in the pages of the New Testament; but the insisting upon *dogmas* in the strict sense of the word,—the statements of creeds, and the decrees of councils, with all their rigid inflexibility, their absence of human sympathy, and their striking contrast to the whole manner and tone of Apostolic teaching.

If so, however, the question is still further narrowed. It is admitted, if so, not only that doctrine lies at the root of all Christian preaching, but that all preaching must express and appeal to the supernatural facts and doctrines which the New Testament reveals, and which are acknowledged to be the springs of the Christian life. Would God, that thus much were admitted, loyally and frankly, in every English pulpit! It still remains, in this view of the subject, to be considered, what is the best mode of presenting doctrine from the pulpit;—a question far narrower indeed than that with which we have begun this paper, but yet, perhaps, of deeper interest to the mass of those here present.

The contrast which undoubtedly exists between the theology of creeds and councils and that of the New Testament is variously regarded as consisting,

1. In a substantive difference as to the doctrine received;

2. In the mode of conceiving doctrine, and the form of expressing it.

As an instance of the first may be mentioned the old accusation brought against what is called the Nicene doctrine of the Trinity, as not to be found in the Bible. The discussion of a point like this is obviously beyond our present reach, and passes altogether into another field of controversy. I mention it only because I think that in some minds the objection to Creeds is not faithfully analysed, and that the objection which is urged against the form is in reality inspired by a dislike of the substance.

The second objection, that the mode in which creeds and councils conceive and express doctrine is different from that of the New Testament and inferior to it, is one which deserves a full and careful examination. It amounts, in fact, to saying that doctrine, not dogma, is the true subject-matter of Christian preaching. Let us examine the terms.

By *Dogma* (as the word is used by modern writers) I understand broadly an authoritative decree, such as were the commands of the Mosaic Law, τὸν νόμον τῶν ἐντολῶν ἐν δόγμασι (Eph. ii. 15); or the decrees of the Council of Jerusalem. As limited by custom to a special subject-matter, it comes to mean Doctrine as defined by authoritative decree of the Church. Doctrine and Dogma are identical, therefore, as to their subject, although not coincident in extent, for there is much doctrine which has not become the subject of dogma. Dogmas are, in short, to quote the words of the late Dr. Baur of Tübingen, "the doctrines of the Christian faith, so far as they are expressed in propositions, in which they exhibit, as far as possible, their defined form of Church teaching. It is impossible, for instance, to speak of the dogma of the Trinity without at the same time thinking of a defined form of that doctrine." I have quoted these words from a quarter not to be suspected of a leaning towards Church teaching, because they are a definition of dogma, and something more. They express shortly what dogma is, and how it arose. It arose, in fact, from that necessity of definition which every branch of human knowledge experiences, and from which the highest is not and cannot be exempt. To infer that theological definition is useless, because the New Testament does not teach by definitions, is like arguing that there can be no value in a grammar, because none was written by Thucydides or by Cicero. It is not the creative spirit but the learner who needs the aid of definition. But in theological as in every other science, more exact definition implies an increase of knowledge. Doubtless, for instance, the earliest Christians, though they held implicitly the doctrine of the Trinity, did not realise, as fully as those who penned the Creed of Nicæa, all that was involved in that great cardinal doctrine. It was by conflict, by discussion, by the necessity of repelling false inferences from the words of Scripture or of the Church, that a more exact definition was at length arrived at. And that exactness of definition, in this as in other cases, is not merely an intellectual acquisition, it is a distinct spiritual gain. It is for us, in its own department, what in another is a richer liturgy or a more spiritual hymnal. It points our devotion with a clearer aim. It enlarges our thoughts of God; it invests Him in our hearts with a fuller and more perfect personality.

The main use, then, of dogma, or theological definition, is threefold:—

1. As a protection to the Church against the encroachment of heresy.

2. As a guide to the theological student.

3. As a religious benefit to the people.

With the first of these uses we have nothing here to do, and with the second only so far as it is intimately connected with the third. But it may be observed, that language is often used which is calculated to disparage, without exactly denying, the value of dogma, as a guide at least to a preacher. It is suggested that the pulpit has lost much by the substitution of rigorously defined teaching for the spirit-stirring appeals of St. Paul, or the simplicity of the Gospel exhortation. As if the great difference between the teaching of St. Paul and our own consisted in his neglect and our employment of exact theological language; or as if it were to be expected that if we would only burn our creeds, and study unfettered the letters of the Apostles and the personal teaching of our Lord, the fervour of apostolic preaching would return, and the glories of the early Church would revive.

This language is, in fact, compounded of a very obvious truth and a very glaring misstatement. If it is meant that spirit-stirring appeals and simple exhortations are more suitable to the pulpit than the terms of an exact theology, the truth of the remark is obvious; but it is (as we shall see more fully presently) in no way inconsistent with strictly dogmatic teaching. If it is meant that such appeals and exhortations cannot be produced by men whose minds are imbued with exact theological thought, and that one secret of St. Paul's fervour is the absence from his own mind of exact theological conception,—I venture to think that the meaning is one which to express clearly is to answer. An exact theologian may indeed not be a fervid or effective preacher, but assuredly, in that case, he would not become one if he could be made to forget his theology.

By the use of dogmatic statement for the general religious benefit of the people, is meant, for our present purpose, the use of it by the preacher, not for his personal guidance, but for the instruction of those whom he addresses.

And this is the part of our subject which requires the closest and most careful attention. For here in fact is presented to us the question of dogmatic preaching in that ultimate form in which it may fairly admit of very different answers from men who are equally alive to the value of exact doctrine. Let us, before we proceed, recapitulate the results at which we have arrived. We have seen,

(1) That the teaching of positive doctrine is of the very essence of Christian preaching.

(2) That it is impossible to teach this doctrine merely in its effects on the life; it cannot be merely implied, it must be expressed.

(3) That doctrine entails dogma in the inevitable progress of things.

(4) That dogma or defined doctrine is not merely inevitable, but valuable, at least to the student of theology.

It remains to be considered whether it is equally valuable to the Christian community at large.: and if so, in what manner, and under what conditions, it is best imparted to them. It is especially to be observed while we do so, that, as we have seen, supernatural facts lie at the very basis of Christianity, and that these must be taught to every Christian congregation; and that on these, and not on vague emotion, is to be built our appeal to the hearts and consciences of men. Now it must be confessed that this being the case, the first presumption is in favour of exact dogmatic teaching. The whole analogy of all secular learning is in its favour. Everywhere the value is acknowledged of exact definition, and of clear summaries of the leading principles of the subject, as the best and surest guide to the beginner, as the stay and the corrector of the master. No reason would appear why it should be otherwise in theology; and it is, I think, well worthy of consideration how far the safety with which we place the Bible in the hands of our people, may not depend on their perfect familiarity with the Creed, acting as an ever-present interpreter, and giving cohesion and unity to the teaching of the Sacred Volume.

Another argument may be derived from the

way in which, as a matter of history, dogmatic statements have arisen. They are an answer to the searching questions which human thought has put to the propounders of Christian doctrine. When these searching questions cease, then perhaps, but not till then, can Christian doctrine be expounded in an undogmatic form. As it is, they must be taught in the face of an inquiring world, and a world which has learnt by long usage to attach a particular meaning to the use or to the absence of certain theological statements. We cannot revoke the past, or will into nothing the history of eighteen centuries.

It will, indeed, be freely admitted by many that the theory of dogmatic teaching is excellent, but that in practice it is open to such serious objections as in fact to involve its failure.

The chief of these admit, I believe, of being summed under three heads:—

1. That it is negative, barren, and unprofitable.

2. That it is essentially a teaching at second-hand, which involves a fatal loss of power.

3. That it tends to sow and perpetuate differences.

The two first of these objections have so far common ground that they both suggest the question, whether they apply to all dogmatic preaching, or only to particular forms of it— whether, in short, they are of force against such preaching altogether, or only as pointing out certain faults, or corruptions, to which it is especially liable.

1. For example, to take the first. When people complain that dogma may inform the head, but cannot warm the heart, or when they say that the natural effect of dogmatic preaching upon the mind is to lead it to think of faith as consisting in the rejection of error, they are mentally identifying dogmatic preaching with controversy. But controversy is not dogma. It is the aspect indeed which dogma presents to its enemies: but to its disciples it wears a far different face. It is, of all things, the most positive and practical. It is instinct with joyous thoughts, and the springs of a holy life.

2. To the second objection, that dogmatic preaching is essentially a second-hand preaching, I should have been glad, had time permitted, to give a fuller consideration. By the objection is meant that the sure tendency of

such preaching is to throw the preacher upon the study of systems of theology, rather than upon the study of the Bible on one side, and of human character on the other.

It is an objection, let me say it frankly, full of weight and importance. The general reply to it is, as I have already hinted, that this tendency is not of the essence of such preaching, it is only an accident and corruption of it. The profoundest theologians have known the best how true it is that *pectus facit theologum*, and that their inspiration must be sought on their knees, from the very fountain-heads of truth. All human theology is at the best but a guide to the study of the Bible. But the danger of losing sight of this is a real and, I am persuaded, a present one. Let me instance a single case. We are contending earnestly for the doctrine of the true Divinity of our Lord, as the one upon which, perhaps more than on any other, the controversies of our day depend. We throw, in our eagerness, into the background His equally true Humanity. Then there appears a work, like the well-known *Ecce Homo*, giving a one-sided and often painful, but vivid, portraiture of the Lord's human life, and it produces an impression far beyond anything which its merits would appear to warrant. The truth is that it thrills to the heart with the power of a forgotten truth, and carries a rebuke to us and to our one-sided preaching. It is but one warning in ten thousand, ever sending back theologians to those sacred pages where truth exhibits herself in seeming contradiction, but without a shade of compromise; and exhibits herself, too, as the parent of holy works, and as the guide of the soul to the presence and throne of its God. In the study of Holy Scripture, and in the mastery of Scriptural Exegesis, we ought to be, as a Church, in the very vanguard of Christendom. So long as it is otherwise—and how far otherwise it is we must confess with shame and sorrow—so long we must offer serious cautions as to the use of a more dogmatic preaching. For until this is attained our preaching, however unexceptionable in doctrine, will be wanting in warmth, and love, and power, and in that true catholicity of tone which no orthodoxy can ensure. Let us hope and pray that no half-hearted timidity—no unwillingness to own what Scriptural interpretation owes to those whose defective faith we lament,—may be permitted to dwarf or retard among us the revival of a profounder study of the Bible. If this, under God's good pleasure, should go hand in hand with the restoration of dogmatic preaching, it may be the instrument in His hands of giving to the Church of England a depth of spiritual life not unequal to the struggle which assuredly lies before her.

3. To the last charge, that dogmatic preaching tends to sow and to perpetuate differences, I own that I am not very careful to answer. There are those, I know, who offer us a millennial repose on the broad basis of the answer of Pilate to Christ. Let truth be an open question, and all the world will be agreed. *Solitudinem faciunt, pacem appellant.* Better than such a peace the keenest and most enduring hostility. Yet I know of one society in which that peace has actually been attained for which these dreamers long. In that society, the loving harmony of which extorted the reluctant praise of her enemies, and which bowed to her gentle sway the civilization of the ancient world,—in the Church of the first three centuries,—there were Liturgies whose strong

dogmatic tones our people would not endure, there was a Discipline based upon doctrines which are now openly derided, there was a Ritual which even in persecution was full of majesty and significance. And this was the Church which has of all human societies the most nearly approached to the ideal of peace among men. Eden, not the desert, is the true land of peace.

October, 1885.

The Clarendon Press, Oxford,
LIST OF SCHOOL BOOKS,

PUBLISHED FOR THE UNIVERSITY BY

HENRY FROWDE,

AT THE OXFORD UNIVERSITY PRESS WAREHOUSE,
AMEN CORNER, LONDON.

※ *All Books are bound in Cloth, unless otherwise described.*

LATIN.

Allen. *An Elementary Latin Grammar.* By J. BARROW ALLEN, M.A. Forty-second Thousand . . . . . . Extra fcap. 8vo. 2s. 6d.

Allen. *Rudimenta Latina.* By the same Author. Extra fcap. 8vo. 2s.

Allen. *A First Latin Exercise Book.* By the same Author. *Fourth Edition.* . . . . Extra fcap. 8vo. 2s. 6d.

Allen. *A Second Latin Exercise Book.* By the same Author.
Extra fcap. 8vo. 3s. 6d.

Jerram. *Anglice Reddenda; or, Easy Extracts, Latin and Greek, for Unseen Translation.* By C. S. JERRAM, M.A. *Fourth Edition.*
Extra fcap. 8vo. 2s. 6d.

Jerram. *Reddenda Minora; or, Easy Passages, Latin and Greek, for Unseen Translation.* For the use of Lower Forms. Composed and selected by C. S. JERRAM, M.A. . . . . . Extra fcap. 8vo. 1s. 6d.

Lee-Warner. *Hints and Helps for Latin Elegiacs.*
Extra fcap. 8vo. 3s. 6d.

Lewis and Short. *A Latin Dictionary,* founded on Andrews' Edition of Freund's Latin Dictionary. By CHARLTON T. LEWIS, Ph.D., and CHARLES SHORT, LL.D. . . . . 4to. 25s.

Nunns. *First Latin Reader.* By T. J. NUNNS, M.A. *Third Edition.*
Extra fcap. 8vo. 2s.

Papillon. *A Manual of Comparative Philology* as applied to the Illustration of Greek and Latin Inflections. By T. L. PAPILLON, M.A. *Third Edition.*
Crown 8vo. 6s.

Ramsay. *Exercises in Latin Prose Composition.* With Introduction, Notes, and Passages of graduated difficulty for Translation into Latin. By G. G. RAMSAY, M.A., Professor of Humanity, Glasgow. *Second Edition.*
Extra fcap. 8vo. 4s. 6d.

Sargent. *Passages for Translation into Latin.* By J. Y. SARGENT, M.A. . . . . Extra fcap. 8vo. 2s. 6d.

Caesar. *The Commentaries* (for Schools). With Notes and Maps. By CHARLES E. MOBERLY, M.A.
    Part I. *The Gallic War. Second Edition.* . . Extra fcap. 8vo. 4s. 6d.
    Part II. *The Civil War.* . . . . . . Extra fcap. 8vo. 3s. 6d.
    The Civil War. Book I. *Second Edition.* . . Extra fcap. 8vo. 2s.

Catulli Veronensis *Carmina Selecta,* secundum recognitionem ROBINSON ELLIS, A.M. . . . . . . Extra fcap. 8vo. 3s. 6d.

Cicero. *Selection of interesting and descriptive passages.* With Notes. By HENRY WALFORD, M.A. In three Parts. *Third Edition.*
Extra fcap. 8vo. 4s. 6d.
    Part I. *Anecdotes from Grecian and Roman History.* . *limp,* 1s. 6d.
    Part II. *Omens and Dreams; Beauties of Nature.* . . *limp,* 1s. 6d.
    Part III. *Rome's Rule of her Provinces.* . . . . *limp,* 1s. 6d.

Cicero. *Pro Cluentio.* With Introduction and Notes. By W. RAMSAY, M.A. Edited by G. G. RAMSAY, M.A. *Second Edition.* Extra fcap. 8vo. 3s. 6d.

Cicero. *Selected Letters* (for Schools). With Notes. By the late C. E. PRICHARD, M.A., and E. R. BERNARD, M.A. *Second Edition.*
Extra fcap. 8vo. 3s.

Cicero. *Select Orations* (for Schools). *First Action against Verres; Oration concerning the command of Gnaeus Pompeius; Oration on behalf of Archias; Ninth Philippic Oration.* With Introduction and Notes. By J. R. KING, M.A. *Second Edition.* . . . . Extra fcap. 8vo. 2s. 6d.

Cicero. *Philippic Orations.* With Notes, &c. by J. R. KING, M.A. *Second Edition.* . . . . 8vo. 10s. 6d.

Cicero. *Select Letters.* With English Introductions, Notes, and Appendices. By ALBERT WATSON, M.A. *Third Edition.* . . . 8vo. 18s.

Cornelius Nepos. With Notes. By OSCAR BROWNING, M.A. *Second Edition.* . . . . . Extra fcap. 8vo. 2s. 6d.

Horace. With a Commentary. Volume I. *The Odes, Carmen Seculare,* and *Epodes.* By EDWARD C. WICKHAM, M.A., Head Master of Wellington College. *Second Edition.* . . . Extra fcap. 8vo. 5s. 6d.

Livy. *Selections* (for Schools). With Notes and Maps. By H. LEE-WARNER, M.A. . . . . Extra fcap. 8vo.
    Part I. *The Caudine Disaster.* . . . . . *limp,* 1s. 6d.
    Part II. *Hannibal's Campaign in Italy.* . . . *limp,* 1s. 6d.
    Part III. *The Macedonian War* . . . . . *limp,* 1s. 6d.

Livy. *Book I.* With Introduction, Historical Examination, and Notes. By J. R. SEELEY, M.A. *Second Edition.* . . . . 8vo. 6s.

Livy. *Books V—VII.* With Introduction and Notes. By A. R. CLUER, B.A. . . . . Extra fcap. 8vo. 3s. 6d.

LIST OF SCHOOL BOOKS.

Livy. *Books XXI—XXIII.* With Introduction and Notes. By M. T. Tatham, M.A. . . . . . Extra fcap. 8vo. *Nearly ready.*

Ovid. *Selections* (for the use of Schools). With Introductions and Notes, and an Appendix on the Roman Calendar. By W. Ramsay, M.A. Edited by G. G. Ramsay, M.A. *Second Edition.* . Extra fcap. 8vo. 5s. 6d.

Ovid. *Tristia,* Book I. Edited by S. G. Owen, B.A.
Extra fcap. 8vo. 3s. 6d.

Persius. *The Satires.* With Translation and Commentary by J. Conington, M.A., edited by H. Nettleship, M.A. *Second Edition.*
8vo. 7s. 6d.

Plautus. *The Trinummus.* With Notes and Introductions. By C. E. Freeman, M.A., Assistant Master of Westminster, and A. Sloman, M.A., Master of the Queen's Scholars of Westminster. . . . Extra fcap. 8vo. 3s.

Pliny. *Selected Letters* (for Schools). With Notes. By the late C. E. Prichard, M.A., and E. R. Bernard, M.A. *Second Edition.*
Extra fcap. 8vo. 3s.

Sallust. *Bellum Catilinarium* and *Jugurthinum.* With Introduction and Notes, by W. W. Capes, M.A. . . . Extra fcap. 8vo. 4s. 6d.

Tacitus. *The Annals.* Books I—IV. Edited, with Introduction and Notes for the use of Schools and Junior Students, by H. Furneaux, M.A.
Extra fcap. 8vo. 5s.

Terence. *Andria.* With Notes and Introductions. By C. E. Freeman, M.A., and A. Sloman, M.A. . . . . . Extra fcap. 8vo. 3s.

Virgil. With Introduction and Notes, by T. L. Papillon, M.A. In Two Volumes. . . . Crown 8vo. 10s. 6d.; Text separately, 4s. 6d.

GREEK.

Chandler. *The Elements of Greek Accentuation* (for Schools). By H. W. Chandler, M.A. *Second Edition.* . Extra fcap. 8vo. 2s. 6d.

Liddell and Scott. *A Greek-English Lexicon,* by Henry George Liddell, D.D., and Robert Scott, D.D. *Seventh Edition.* . 4to. 36s.

Liddell and Scott. *A Greek-English Lexicon,* abridged from Liddell and Scott's 4to. edition, chiefly for the use of Schools. *Twenty-first Edition.*
Square 12mo. 7s. 6d.

Veitch. *Greek Verbs, Irregular and Defective:* their forms, meaning, and quantity; embracing all the Tenses used by Greek writers, with references to the passages in which they are found. By W. Veitch, LL.D. *Fourth Edition.*
Crown 8vo. 10s. 6d.

Wordsworth. *Graecae Grammaticae Rudimenta in usum Scholarum.* Auctore Carolo Wordsworth, D.C.L. *Nineteenth Edition.* . 12mo. 4s.

Wordsworth. *A Greek Primer, for the use of beginners in that Language.* By the Right Rev. Charles Wordsworth, D.C.L., Bishop of St. Andrew's. *Seventh Edition.* . . . Extra fcap. 8vo. 1s. 6d.

Wright. *The Golden Treasury of Ancient Greek Poetry;* being a Collection of the finest passages in the Greek Classic Poets, with Introductory Notices and Notes. By R. S. WRIGHT, M.A. . . Extra fcap. 8vo. 8s. 6d.

Wright and Shadwell. *A Golden Treasury of Greek Prose;* being a Collection of the finest passages in the principal Greek Prose Writers, with Introductory Notices and Notes. By R. S. WRIGHT, M.A., and J. E. L. SHADWELL, M.A. . . . . Extra fcap. 8vo. 4s. 6d.

A SERIES OF GRADUATED READERS.—

First Greek Reader. By W. G. RUSHBROOKE, M.L., Second Classical Master at the City of London School. *Second Edition.*
Extra fcap. 8vo. 2s. 6d.

Second Greek Reader. By A. M. BELL, M.A.
Extra fcap. 8vo. 3s. 6d.

Third Greek Reader. In Preparation.

Fourth Greek Reader; being Specimens of Greek Dialects. With Introductions and Notes. By W. W. MERRY, M.A., Rector of Lincoln College. . . . . Extra fcap. 8vo. 4s. 6d.

Fifth Greek Reader. Selections from Greek Epic and Dramatic Poetry, with Introductions and Notes. By EVELYN ABBOTT, M.A.
Extra fcap. 8vo. 4s. 6d.

THE GREEK TESTAMENT.—

Evangelia Sacra Graece. . . . Fcap. 8vo. *limp,* 1s. 6d.

The Greek Testament, with the Readings adopted by the Revisers of the Authorised Version.
Fcap. 8vo. 4s. 6d.; or on writing paper, with wide margin, 15s.

Novum Testamentum Graece juxta Exemplar Millianum.
18mo. 2s. 6d.; or on writing paper, with large margin, 9s.

Novum Testamentum Graece. Accedunt parallela S. Scripturae loca, necnon vetus capitulorum notatio et canones Eusebii. Edidit CAROLUS LLOYD, S.T.P.R., necnon Episcopus Oxoniensis.
18mo. 3s.; or on writing paper, with large margin, 10s. 6d.

The New Testament in Greek and English. Edited by E. CARDWELL, D.D. . . . . 2 vols. crown 8vo. 6s.

Outlines of Textual Criticism applied to the New Testament. By C. E. HAMMOND, M.A. *Fourth Edition.* . . Extra fcap. 8vo. 3s. 6d.

Aeschylus. *Agamemnon.* With Introduction and Notes, by ARTHUR SIDGWICK, M.A. *Second Edition.* . . . . . Extra fcap. 8vo. 3s.

Aeschylus. *The Choephoroi.* With Introduction and Notes, by the same Editor. . . . . Extra fcap. 8vo. 3s.

Aeschylus. *Prometheus Bound.* With Introduction and Notes, by A. O. PRICKARD, M.A. *Second Edition.* . . . Extra fcap. 8vo. 2s.

Aristophanes. *The Clouds.* With Introduction and Notes, by W. W. MERRY, M.A. *Second Edition.* . . . . . Extra fcap. 8vo. 2s.

Aristophanes. *The Acharnians.* By the same Editor.
Extra fcap. 8vo. 2s.

Aristophanes. *The Frogs.* By the same Editor.
Extra fcap. 8vo. 2s.

Cebes. *Tabula.* With Introduction and Notes, by C. S. JERRAM, M.A.
Extra fcap. 8vo. 2s. 6d.

Demosthenes and Aeschines. *The Orations of Demosthenes and Æschines on the Crown.* With Introductory Essays and Notes. By G. A. SIMCOX, M.A., and W. H. SIMCOX, M.A. . . . . . . 8vo. 12s.

Euripides. *Alcestis.* By C. S. JERRAM, M.A. Extra fcap. 8vo. 2s. 6d.

Euripides. *Helena.* For Upper and Middle Forms. By the same Editor. . . . . Extra fcap. 8vo. 3s.

Euripides. *Iphigenia in Tauris.* With Introduction and Notes. By the same Editor. . . . . Extra fcap. 8vo. 3s.

Herodotus. *Selections,* edited, with Introduction, Notes, and a Map, by W. W. MERRY, M.A. . . . . . Extra fcap. 8vo. 2s. 6d.

Homer. *Iliad,* Books I-XII. With an Introduction, a brief Homeric Grammar, and Notes. By D. B. MONRO, M.A. Extra fcap. 8vo. 6s.

Homer. *Iliad,* Book I. By the same Editor. *Third Edition.*
Extra fcap. 8vo. 2s.

Homer. *Iliad,* Books VI and XXI. With Notes, &c. By HERBERT HAILSTONE, M.A. . . . . . Extra fcap. 8vo. 1s. 6d. each.

Homer. *Odyssey,* Books I-XII. By W. W. MERRY, M.A. *Thirty-second Thousand.* . . . . Extra fcap. 8vo. 4s. 6d.

Homer: *Odyssey,* Books XIII-XXIV. By the same Editor. *Second Edition.* . . . . Extra fcap. 8vo. 5s.

Homer. *Odyssey,* Book II. By the same Editor. Extra fcap. 8vo. 1s. 6d.

Lucian. *Vera Historia.* By C. S. JERRAM, M.A. *Second Edition.*
Extra fcap. 8vo. 1s. 6d.

Plato. *The Apology.* With a revised Text and English Notes, and a Digest of Platonic Idioms, by JAMES RIDDELL, M.A. . . 8vo. 8s. 6d.

Plato. *Selections* (including the whole of the *Apology* and *Crito*). With Introductions and Notes by J. PURVES, M.A., and a Preface by B. JOWETT, M.A.
Extra fcap. 8vo. 6s. 6d.

Sophocles. In Single Plays, with English Notes, &c. By LEWIS CAMPBELL, M.A., Professor of Greek in the University of St. Andrew's, and EVELYN ABBOTT, M.A. . . . . . Extra fcap. 8vo. *limp.*
   Oedipus Tyrannus, Philoctetes. New and Revised Edition, 2s. each.
      Oedipus Coloneus, Antigone. 1s. 9d. each.
         Ajax,   Electra,   Trachiniae. 2s. each.

Sophocles. *Oedipus Rex:* Dindorf's Text, with Notes by W. BASIL JONES, D.D., Lord Bishop of S. David's. . Extra fcap. 8vo. *limp*, 1s. 6d.

Theocritus. Edited, with Notes, by H. KYNASTON, D.D. (late SNOW), Head Master of Cheltenham College. *Third Edition.*
Extra fcap. 8vo. 4s. 6d.

Xenophon. *Easy Selections* (for Junior Classes). With a Vocabulary, Notes, and Map. By J. S. PHILLPOTTS, B.C.L., Head Master of Bedford School, and C. S. JERRAM, M.A. *Third Edition.* . Extra fcap. 8vo. 3s. 6d.

Xenophon. *Selections* (for Schools). With Notes and Maps. By J. S. PHILLPOTTS, B.C.L. *Fourth Edition.* . . Extra fcap. 8vo. 3s. 6d.

Xenophon. *Anabasis*, Book I. With Notes and Map. By J. MARSHALL, M.A., Rector of the High School, Edinburgh. Extra fcap. 8vo. *Nearly ready.*

Xenophon. *Anabasis*, Book II. With Notes and Map. By C. S. JERRAM, M.A. . . . . Extra fcap. 8vo. 2s.

Xenophon. *Cyropaedia*, Books IV, V. With Introduction and Notes, by C. BIGG, D.D. . . . . . . Extra fcap. 8vo. 2s. 6d.

ENGLISH.

Reading Books.

—— *A First Reading Book.* By MARIE EICHENS of Berlin; edited by ANNE J. CLOUGH. . . . . Extra fcap. 8vo. *stiff covers*, 4d.

—— *Oxford Reading Book*, Part I. For Little Children.
Extra fcap. 8vo. *stiff covers*, 6d.

—— *Oxford Reading Book*, Part II. For Junior Classes.
Extra fcap. 8vo. *stiff covers*, 6d.

Tancock. *An Elementary English Grammar and Exercise Book.* By O. W. TANCOCK, M.A., Head Master of King Edward VI's School, Norwich. *Second Edition.* . . . . . . Extra fcap. 8vo. 1s. 6d.

Tancock. *An English Grammar and Reading Book*, for Lower Forms in Classical Schools. By O. W. TANCOCK, M.A. *Fourth Edition.*
Extra fcap. 8vo. 3s. 6d.

Earle. *The Philology of the English Tongue.* By J. EARLE, M.A., Professor of Anglo-Saxon. *Third Edition.* . . Extra fcap. 8vo. 7s. 6d.

Earle. *A Book for the Beginner in Anglo-Saxon.* By the same Author. *Third Edition.* . . . . Extra fcap. 8vo. 2s. 6d.

Sweet. *An Anglo-Saxon Primer, with Grammar, Notes, and Glossary.* By HENRY SWEET, M.A. *Third Edition.* . . Extra fcap. 8vo. 2s. 6d.

Sweet. *An Anglo-Saxon Reader.* In Prose and Verse. With Grammatical Introduction, Notes, and Glossary. By the same Author. *Fourth Edition, Revised and Enlarged.* . . . . Extra fcap. 8vo. 8s. 6d.

Sweet. *Anglo-Saxon Reading Primers.*
  I. *Selected Homilies of Ælfric.* . Extra fcap. 8vo. *stiff covers*, 1s. 6d.
  II. *Extracts from Alfred's Orosius.* Extra fcap. 8vo. *stiff covers*, 1s. 6d.

Sweet. *First Middle English Primer, with Grammar and Glossary.* By the same Author. . . . . . . Extra fcap. 8vo. 2s.

Morris and Skeat. *Specimens of Early English.* A New and Revised Edition. With Introduction, Notes, and Glossarial Index. By R. MORRIS, LL.D., and W. W. SKEAT, M.A.
  Part I. From Old English Homilies to King Horn (A.D. 1150 to A.D. 1300). *Second Edition.* . . . . . . Extra fcap. 8vo. 9s.
  Part II. From Robert of Gloucester to Gower (A.D. 1298 to A.D. 1393). *Second Edition.* . . . . Extra fcap. 8vo. 7s. 6d.

Skeat. *Specimens of English Literature,* from the 'Ploughmans Crede' to the 'Shepheardes Calender' (A.D. 1394 to A.D. 1579). With Introduction, Notes, and Glossarial Index. By W. W. SKEAT, M.A.
Extra fcap. 8vo. 7s. 6d.

Typical Selections from the best English Writers, with Introductory Notices. *Second Edition.* In Two Volumes. Vol. I. Latimer to Berkeley. Vol. II. Pope to Macaulay. . . Extra fcap. 8vo. 3s. 6d. each.

A SERIES OF ENGLISH CLASSICS.—

Langland. *The Vision of William concerning Piers the Plowman,* by WILLIAM LANGLAND. Edited by W. W. SKEAT, M.A. *Third Edition.*
Extra fcap. 8vo. 4s. 6d.

Chaucer. I. *The Prologue to the Canterbury Tales; The Knightes Tale; The Nonne Prestes Tale.* Edited by R. MORRIS, LL.D. *Fifty-first Thousand.* . . . . Extra fcap. 8vo. 2s. 6d.

Chaucer. II. *The Prioresses Tale; Sir Thopas; The Monkes Tale; The Clerkes Tale; The Squieres Tale, &c.* Edited by W. W. SKEAT, M.A. *Second Edition.* . . . . . . Extra fcap. 8vo. 4s. 6d.

Chaucer. III. *The Tale of the Man of Lawe; The Pardoneres Tale; The Second Nonnes Tale; The Chanouns Yemannes Tale.* By the same Editor. *Second Edition.* . . . . . Extra fcap. 8vo. 4s. 6d.

Gamelyn, The Tale of. Edited by W. W. SKEAT, M.A.
Extra fcap. 8vo. *stiff covers,* 1s. 6d.

Wycliffe. *The New Testament in English,* according to the Version by JOHN WYCLIFFE, about A.D. 1380. and Revised by JOHN PURVEY, about A.D. 1388. With Introduction and Glossary by W. W. SKEAT, M.A.
Extra fcap. 8vo. 6s.

Wycliffe. *The Books of Job, Psalms, Proverbs, Ecclesiastes, and the Song of Solomon:* according to the Wycliffite Version made by NICHOLAS DE HEREFORD, about A.D. 1381. and Revised by JOHN PURVEY, about A.D. 1388. With Introduction and Glossary by W. W. SKEAT, M.A. Extra fcap. 8vo. 3s. 6d.

Spenser. *The Faery Queene.* Books I and II. Edited by G. W. KITCHIN, D.D.
  Book I. *Tenth Edition.* . . . . . Extra fcap. 8vo. 2s. 6d.
  Book II. *Sixth Edition.* . . . . Extra fcap. 8vo. 2s. 6d.

Hooker. *Ecclesiastical Polity.* Book I. Edited by R. W. CHURCH, M.A., Dean of St. Paul's. *Second Edition.* . . . Extra fcap. 8vo. 2*s.*

Marlowe and Greene.—MARLOWE'S *Tragical History of Dr. Faustus,* and GREENE'S *Honourable History of Friar Bacon and Friar Bungay.* Edited by A. W. WARD, M.A. . . . . Extra fcap. 8vo. 5*s.* 6*d.*

Marlowe. *Edward II.* Edited by O. W. TANCOCK, M.A.
Extra fcap. 8vo. 3*s.*

Shakespeare. Select Plays. Edited by W. G. CLARK, M.A., and W. ALDIS WRIGHT, M.A. . . . . Extra fcap. 8vo. *stiff covers.*

The Merchant of Venice. 1*s.*   *Macbeth.* 1*s.* 6*d.*
Richard the Second. 1*s.* 6*d.*   *Hamlet.* 2*s.*

Edited by W. ALDIS WRIGHT, M.A.

The Tempest. 1*s.* 6*d.*   *Coriolanus.* 2*s.* 6*d.*
As You Like It. 1*s.* 6*d.*   *Richard the Third.* 2*s.* 6*d.*
A Midsummer Night's Dream. 1*s.* 6*d.*   *Henry the Fifth.* 2*s.*
Twelfth Night. 1*s.* 6*d.*   *King John.* In the Press.
Julius Cæsar. 2*s.*   *King Lear.* 1*s.* 6*d.*

Shakespeare as a Dramatic Artist; *a popular Illustration of the Principles of Scientific Criticism.* By RICHARD G. MOULTON, M.A.
Crown 8vo. 5*s.*

Bacon. I. *Advancement of Learning.* Edited by W. ALDIS WRIGHT, M.A. *Second Edition.* . . . . Extra fcap. 8vo. 4*s.* 6*d.*

Bacon. II. *The Essays.* With Introduction and Notes. *In Preparation.*

Milton. I. *Areopagitica.* With Introduction and Notes. By JOHN W. HALES, M.A. *Third Edition.* . . . . Extra fcap. 8vo. 3*s.*

Milton. II. *Poems.* Edited by R. C. BROWNE, M.A. 2 vols. *Fifth Edition.* . . Extra fcap. 8vo. 6*s.* 6*d.* Sold separately, Vol. I. 4*s.*; Vol. II. 3*s.*

In paper covers :—

Lycidas, 3*d.*   *L'Allegro,* 3*d.*   *Il Penseroso,* 4*d.*   *Comus,* 6*d.*
Samson Agonistes, 6*d.*

Milton. III. *Samson Agonistes.* Edited with Introduction and Notes by JOHN CHURTON COLLINS. . . . Extra fcap. 8vo. *stiff covers,* 1*s.*

Bunyan. I. *The Pilgrim's Progress, Grace Abounding, Relation of the Imprisonment of Mr. John Bunyan.* Edited, with Biographical Introduction and Notes, by E. VENABLES, M.A. . . . Extra fcap. 8vo. 5*s.*

Bunyan. II. *Holy War, &c.* By the same Editor.   *In the Press.*

Dryden. *Select Poems.—Stanzas on the Death of Oliver Cromwell; Astræa Redux; Annus Mirabilis; Absalom and Achitophel; Religio Laici; The Hind and the Panther.* Edited by W. D. CHRISTIE, M.A.
Extra fcap. 8vo. 3*s.* 6*d.*

LIST OF SCHOOL BOOKS.

Locke's *Conduct of the Understanding.* Edited, with Introduction, Notes, &c. by T. FOWLER, M.A. *Second Edition.* . . Extra fcap. 8vo. 2s.

Addison. *Selections from Papers in the 'Spectator.'* With Notes. By T. ARNOLD, M.A. . . . . . . Extra fcap. 8vo. 4s. 6d.

Steele. *Selected Essays from the Tatler, Spectator, and Guardian.* By AUSTIN DOBSON. . . Extra fcap. 8vo. 5s. *In white Parchment,* 7s. 6d.

Berkeley. *Select Works of Bishop Berkeley,* with an Introduction and Notes, by A. C. FRASER, LL.D. *Third Edition.* . . Crown 8vo. 7s. 6d.

Pope. I. *Essay on Man.* Edited by MARK PATTISON, B.D. *Sixth Edition.* . . . . Extra fcap. 8vo. 1s. 6d.

Pope. II. *Satires and Epistles.* By the same Editor. *Second Edition.*
Extra fcap. 8vo. 2s.

Parnell. *The Hermit.* . . . . . . *Paper covers,* 2d.

Johnson. I. *Rasselas; Lives of Dryden and Pope.* Edited by ALFRED MILNES, M.A. . . . . . Extra fcap. 8vo. 4s. 6d.
Lives of Pope and Dryden. . . . . . *Stiff covers,* 2s. 6d.

Johnson. II. *Vanity of Human Wishes.* With Notes, by E. J. PAYNE, M.A. . . . . *Paper covers,* 4d.

Gray. *Selected Poems.* Edited by EDMUND GOSSE.
Extra fcap. 8vo. *Stiff covers,* 1s. 6d. *In white Parchment,* 3s.

Gray. *Elegy, and Ode on Eton College.* . . *Paper covers,* 2d.

Goldsmith. *The Deserted Village.* . . . *Paper covers,* 2d.

Cowper. I. *The Didactic Poems of* 1782, with Selections from the Minor Pieces, A.D. 1779-1783. Edited by H. T. GRIFFITH, B.A.
Extra fcap. 8vo. 3s.

Cowper. II. *The Task, with Tirocinium,* and Selections from the Minor Poems, A.D. 1784-1799. By the same Editor. *Second Edition.*
Extra fcap. 8vo. 3s.

Burke. I. *Thoughts on the Present Discontents; the two Speeches on America.* Edited by E. J. PAYNE, M.A. *Second Edition.*
Extra fcap. 8vo. 4s. 6d.

Burke. II. *Reflections on the French Revolution.* By the same Editor. *Second Edition.* . . . . . . Extra fcap. 8vo. 5s.

Burke. III. *Four Letters on the Proposals for Peace with the Regicide Directory of France.* By the same Editor. *Second Edition.*
Extra fcap. 8vo. 5s.

Keats. *Hyperion,* Book I. With Notes, by W. T. ARNOLD, B.A.
Paper covers, 4d.

Byron. *Childe Harold.* With Introduction and Notes, by H. F. TOZER, M.A. . . . . Extra fcap. 8vo. *Nearly ready.*

Scott. *Lay of the Last Minstrel.* Introduction and Canto I, with Preface and Notes by W. MINTO, M.A. . . . . *Paper covers,* 6d.

FRENCH AND ITALIAN.

Brachet. *Etymological Dictionary of the French Language,* with a Preface on the Principles of French Etymology. Translated into English by G. W. KITCHIN, D.D., Dean of Winchester. *Third Edition.*
Crown 8vo. 7s. 6d.

Brachet. *Historical Grammar of the French Language.* Translated into English by G. W. KITCHIN, D.D. *Fourth Edition.*
Extra fcap. 8vo. 3s. 6d.

Saintsbury. *Primer of French Literature.* By GEORGE SAINTSBURY, M.A. *Second Edition.* . . . . . Extra fcap. 8vo. 2s.

Saintsbury. *Short History of French Literature.* By the same Author. . . . . Crown 8vo. 10s. 6d.

Saintsbury. *Specimens of French Literature.* Crown 8vo. 9s.

Beaumarchais. *Le Barbier de Séville.* With Introduction and Notes by AUSTIN DOBSON. . . . . . Extra fcap. 8vo. 2s. 6d.

Blouët. *L'Éloquence de la Chaire et de la Tribune Françaises.* Edited by PAUL BLOUËT, B.A. (Univ. Gallic.). Vol. I. *French Sacred Oratory.*
Extra fcap. 8vo. 2s. 6d.

Corneille. *Horace.* With Introduction and Notes by GEORGE SAINTSBURY, M.A. . . , . . . Extra fcap. 8vo. 2s. 6d.

Corneille. *Cinna.*
Molière. *Les Femmes Savantes.*
In one volume, with Introduction and Notes by GUSTAVE MASSON, B.A.
Extra fcap. 8vo. 2s. 6d.

Masson. *Louis XIV and his Contemporaries;* as described in Extracts from the best Memoirs of the Seventeenth Century. With English Notes, Genealogical Tables, &c. By GUSTAVE MASSON, B.A. Extra fcap. 8vo. 2s. 6d.

Molière. *Les Précieuses Ridicules.* With Introduction and Notes by ANDREW LANG, M.A. . . . . . Extra fcap. 8vo. 1s. 6d.

Molière. *Les Fourberies de Scapin.*
Racine. *Athalie.*
With Voltaire's Life of Molière. By GUSTAVE MASSON, B.A.
Extra fcap. 8vo. 2s. 6d.

Molière. *Les Fourberies de Scapin.* With Voltaire's Life of Molière. By GUSTAVE MASSON, B.A. . . Extra fcap. 8vo. *stiff covers,* 1s. 6d.

Musset. *On ne badine pas avec l'Amour,* and *Fantasio.* With Introduction, Notes, etc., by WALTER HERRIES POLLOCK. Extra fcap. 8vo. 2s.

LIST OF SCHOOL BOOKS.

NOVELETTES :—

Xavier de Maistre.	*Voyage autour de ma Chambre.*	⎫ By Gustave
Madame de Duras.	*Ourika.*	⎪ Masson, B.A.
Fiévée.	*La Dot de Suzette.*	⎬ *2nd Edition.*
Edmond About.	*Les Jumeaux de l' Hôtel Corneille.*	⎪ Ext. fcap. 8vo.
Rodolphe Töpffer.	*Mésaventures d'un Écolier.*	⎭ 2s. 6d.

Quinet. *Lettres à sa Mère.* Edited by G. SAINTSBURY, M.A.
　　　　　　　　　　　　　　　　　　　　Extra fcap. 8vo. 2s.

Racine.　*Andromaque.* ⎱ With Louis Racine's Life of his Father. By
Corneille. *Le Menteur.* ⎰ 　Gustave Masson, B.A.
　　　　　　　　　　　　　　　　　　Extra fcap. 8vo. 2s. 6d.

Regnard. . . . *Le Joueur.* ⎱ By Gustave Masson, B.A.
Brueys and Palaprat. *Le Grondeur.* ⎰ 　Extra fcap. 8vo. 2s. 6d.

Sainte-Beuve. *Selections from the Causeries du Lundi.* Edited by
　G. SAINTSBURY, M.A. . . . . . . Extra fcap. 8vo. 2s.

Sévigné. *Selections from the Correspondence of* **Madame de Sévigné**
　and her chief Contemporaries. Intended more especially for Girls' Schools. By
　GUSTAVE MASSON, B.A. . . . . . Extra fcap. 8vo. 3s.

Voltaire. *Mérope.* Edited by G. SAINTSBURY, M.A. Extra fcap. 8vo. 2s.

Dante. *Selections from the 'Inferno.'* With Introduction and Notes,
　by H. B. COTTERILL, B.A. . . .. . . Extra fcap. 8vo. 4s. 6d.

Tasso. *La Gerusalemme Liberata.* Cantos i, ii. With Introduction
　and Notes, by the same Editor. . . . Extra fcap. 8vo. 2s. 6d.

GERMAN, &c.

Buchheim. *Modern German Reader.* A Graduated Collection of
　Prose Extracts from Modern German writers. Edited by C. A. BUCHHEIM,
　Phil. Doc.
　Part I. With English Notes, a Grammatical Appendix, and a complete
　　Vocabulary. *Fourth Edition.* . . . Extra fcap. 8vo. 2s. 6d.
　Part II. In the Press.　Part III. In preparation.

Lange. *The Germans at Home*; a Practical Introduction to German
　Conversation with an Appendix containing the Essentials of German Grammar.
　By HERMANN LANGE. *Second Edition.* . . . . 8vo. 2s. 6d.

Lange. *The German Manual*; a German Grammar, a Reading
　Book, and a Handbook of German Conversation. By the same Author.
　　　　　　　　　　　　　　　　　　　　　　　8vo. 7s. 6d.

Lange. *A Grammar of the German Language,* being a reprint of the
　Grammar contained in *The German Manual.* By the same Author. 8vo. 3s. 6d.

Lange. *German Composition*; a Theoretical and Practical Guide to
　the Art of Translating English Prose into German. By the same Author.
　　　　　　　　　　　　　　　　　　　　　　　8vo. 4s. 6d.

Goethe. *Egmont.* With a Life of Goethe, etc. Edited by C. A. Buchheim, Phil. Doc. *Third Edition.* . . . Extra fcap. 8vo. 3s.

Goethe. *Iphigenie auf Tauris.* A Drama. With a Critical Introduction and Notes. Edited by C. A. Buchheim, Phil. Doc. *Second Edition.* Extra fcap. 8vo. 3s.

Heine's *Prosa*, being Selections from his Prose Works. Edited with English Notes, etc., by C. A. Buchheim, Phil. Doc. Extra fcap. 8vo. 4s. 6d.

Lessing. *Laokoon.* With Introduction, Notes, etc. By A. Hamann, Phil. Doc., M.A. . . . . Extra fcap. 8vo. 4s. 6d.

Lessing. *Minna von Barnhelm.* A Comedy. With a Life of Lessing, Critical Analysis, Complete Commentary, etc. Edited by C. A. Buchheim, Phil. Doc. *Fourth Edition.* . . Extra fcap. 8vo. 3s. 6d.

Lessing. *Nathan der Weise.* With English Notes, etc. Edited by C. A. Buchheim, Phil. Doc. . . . . . Extra fcap. 8vo. 4s. 6d.

Schiller's *Historische Skizzen:—Egmonts Leben und Tod,* and *Belagerung von Antwerpen.* Edited by C. A. Buchheim, Phil. Doc. *Third Edition, Revised and Enlarged, with a Map.* . Extra fcap. 8vo. 2s. 6d.

Schiller. *Wilhelm Tell.* With a Life of Schiller; an Historical and Critical Introduction, Arguments, a Complete Commentary, and Map. Edited by C. A. Buchheim, Phil. Doc. *Sixth Edition.* . Extra fcap. 8vo. 3s. 6d.

Schiller. *Wilhelm Tell.* Edited by C. A. Buchheim, Phil. Doc. *School Edition.* With Map. . . . . . Extra fcap. 8vo. 2s.

Schiller. *Wilhelm Tell.* Translated into English Verse by E. Massie, M.A. . . . . Extra fcap. 8vo. 5s.

GOTHIC AND ICELANDIC.

Skeat. *The Gospel of St. Mark in Gothic.* Edited by W. W. Skeat, M.A. . . . . Extra fcap. 8vo. 4s.

Vigfusson and Powell. *An Icelandic Prose Reader*, with Notes, Grammar, and Glossary. By Gudbrand Vigfusson, M.A., and F. York Powell, M.A. . . . . . . Extra fcap. 8vo. 10s. 6d.

MATHEMATICS AND PHYSICAL SCIENCE.

Hamilton and Ball. *Book-keeping.* By Sir R. G. C. Hamilton, K.C.B., Under-Secretary for Ireland, and John Ball (of the firm of Quilter, Ball, & Co.). *New and Enlarged Edition* . . Extra fcap. 8vo. 2s.

Hensley. *Figures made Easy: a first Arithmetic Book.* By Lewis Hensley, M.A. . . . . Crown 8vo. 6d.

Hensley. *Answers to the Examples in Figures made Easy,* together with 2000 additional Examples formed from the Tables in the same, with Answers. By the same Author. . . . . . Crown 8vo. 1s.

LIST OF SCHOOL BOOKS. 13

Hensley. *The Scholar's Arithmetic;* with Answers to the Examples. By the same Author. . . . . . . Crown 8vo. 4s. 6d.

Hensley. *The Scholar's Algebra.* An Introductory work on Algebra. By the same Author. . . . . . . Crown 8vo. 4s. 6d.

Baynes. *Lessons on Thermodynamics.* By R. E. BAYNES, M.A., Lee's Reader in Physics. . . . . . . Crown 8vo. 7s. 6d.

Donkin. *Acoustics.* By W. F. DONKIN, M.A., F.R.S. *Second Edition.* Crown 8vo. 7s. 6d.

Euclid. Edited by C. J. NIXON, M.A., Royal Academical Institution, Belfast. . . . . . . Extra fcap. 8vo. *Nearly ready.*

Harcourt and Madan. *Exercises in Practical Chemistry.* Vol. I. *Elementary Exercises.* By A. G. VERNON HARCOURT, M.A.: and H. G. MADAN, M.A. *Third Edition.* Revised by H. G. Madan, M.A. Crown 8vo. 9s.

Madan. *Tables of Qualitative Analysis.* Arranged by H. G. MADAN, M.A. . . . . Large 4to. 4s. 6d.

Maxwell. *An Elementary Treatise on Electricity.* By J. CLERK MAXWELL, M.A., F.R.S. Edited by W. GARNETT, M.A. Demy 8vo. 7s. 6d.

Stewart. *A Treatise on Heat,* with numerous Woodcuts and Diagrams. By BALFOUR STEWART, LL.D., F.R.S., Professor of Natural Philosophy in Owens College, Manchester. *Fourth Edition.* . Extra fcap. 8vo. 7s. 6d.

Vernon-Harcourt. *A Treatise on Rivers and Canals,* relating to the Control and Improvement of Rivers, and the Design, Construction, and Development of Canals. By LEVESON FRANCIS VERNON-HARCOURT, M.A., M.I.C.E. 2 vols. (Vol. I, Text. Vol. II, Plates.) . . . 8vo. 21s.

Vernon-Harcourt. *Harbours and Docks;* their Physical Features, History, Construction, Equipment, and Maintenance. By the same Author. 2 vols. (Vol. I, Text. Vol. II, Plates.) . . . . 8vo. 25s.

Williamson. *Chemistry for Students.* By A. W. WILLIAMSON, Phil. Doc., F.R.S., Professor of Chemistry, University College London. *A new Edition with Solutions.* . . . . . Extra fcap. 8vo. 8s. 6d.

HISTORY, &c.

Freeman. *A Short History of the Norman Conquest of England.* By E. A. FREEMAN, M.A. *Second Edition.* . Extra fcap. 8vo. 2s. 6d.

George. *Genealogical Tables illustrative of Modern History.* By H. B. GEORGE, M.A. *Second Edition, Revised and Enlarged.* Small 4to. 12s.

Kitchin. *A History of France.* With Numerous Maps, Plans, and Tables. By G. W. KITCHIN, D.D., Dean of Winchester. Three vols. Crown 8vo. 31s. 6d.

    Vol. 1. To the Year 1453. *Second Edition.* . . . . . 10s. 6d.
    Vol. 2. From 1453 to 1624. . . . . 10s. 6d.
    Vol. 3. From 1624 to 1793. . . . . 10s. 6d.

Rawlinson. *A Manual of Ancient History.* By GEORGE RAWLINSON, M.A.; Camden Professor of Ancient History. *Second Edition.*
Demy 8vo. 14s.

Rogers. *A Manual of Political Economy,* for the use of Schools. By J. E. THOROLD ROGERS, M.P. *Third Edition.* Extra fcap. 8vo. 4s. 6d.

Stubbs. *The Constitutional History of England, in its Origin and Development.* By WILLIAM STUBBS, D.D., Lord Bishop of Chester. Three vols. . . . . Crown 8vo. each 12s.

Stubbs. *Select Charters and other Illustrations of English Constitutional History,* from the Earliest Times to the Reign of Edward I. Arranged and edited by W. STUBBS, D.D. *Fourth Edition.* Crown 8vo. 8s. 6d.

Stubbs. *Magna Carta*: a careful reprint. . . . 4to. *stitched*, 1s.

ART.

Hullah. *The Cultivation of the Speaking Voice.* By JOHN HULLAH.
Extra fcap. 8vo. 2s. 6d.

Maclaren. *A System of Physical Education: Theoretical and Practical.* With 346 Illustrations drawn by A. MACDONALD, of the Oxford School of Art. By ARCHIBALD MACLAREN, the Gymnasium, Oxford. *Second Edition.*
Extra fcap. 8vo. 7s. 6d.

Troutbeck and Dale. *A Music Primer for Schools.* By J. TROUTBECK, M.A., Music Master in Westminster School, and R. F. DALE, M.A., B. Mus., Assistant Master in Westminster School. . Crown 8vo. 1s. 6d.

Tyrwhitt. *A Handbook of Pictorial Art.* By R. St. J. TYRWHITT, M.A. With coloured Illustrations, Photographs, and a chapter on Perspective by A. MACDONALD. *Second Edition.* . . . 8vo. *half morocco*, 18s.

Student's Handbook to the University and Colleges of Oxford. *Eighth Edition.* . . . . Extra fcap. 8vo. 2s. 6d.

Helps to the Study of the Bible, taken from the *Oxford Bible for Teachers,* comprising Summaries of the several Books, with copious Explanatory Notes and Tables illustrative of Scripture History and the Characteristics of Bible Lands; with a complete Index of Subjects, a Concordance, a Dictionary of Proper Names, and a series of Maps. . . . Crown 8vo. 3s. 6d.

☞ *All communications relating to Books included in this List, and offers of new Books and new Editions, should be addressed to*

THE SECRETARY TO THE DELEGATES,
CLARENDON PRESS,
OXFORD.

BOOKS FOR SCHOOL LIBRARIES.

An Etymological Dictionary of the English Language, arranged on an Historical Basis. By W. W. SKEAT, M.A. Second Edition. 2*l.* 4*s.*

Shakespeare as a Dramatic Artist. By R. G. MOULTON, M.A. 5*s.*

English Plant Names, from the tenth to the fifteenth Century. By J. EARLE, M.A. 5*s.*

Baedae Historia Ecclesiastica. Edited by G. H. MOBERLY, M.A. 10*s.* 6*d.*

Chapters of Early English Church History. By W. BRIGHT, D.D. 12*s.*

History of the Norman Conquest of England: its Causes and Results. By E. A. FREEMAN, D.C.L. In 6 vols. 5*l.* 9*s.* 6*d.*

The Reign of William Rufus and the Accession of Henry the First. By E. A. FREEMAN, D.C.L. In 2 vols. 1*l.* 16*s.*

Fuller's Church History of Britain. Edited by J. S. BREWER, M.A. In 6 vols. 1*l.* 19*s.*

Burnet's History of the Reformation of the Church of England. New Edition, revised by N. POCOCK, M.A. In 7 vols. 1*l.* 10*s.*

Clarendon's History of the Rebellion and Civil Wars in England, together with his Life, including a Continuation of his History. 1*l.* 2*s.*

A History of England, principally in the Seventeenth Century. Translation edited by G. W. KITCHIN, D.D., and C. W. BOASE, M.A. In 6 vols. 3*l.* 3*s.*

A History of Greece, B.C. 146 to A.D. 1864. By GEORGE FINLAY, LL.D. New Edition, by H. F. TOZER, M.A. In 7 vols. 3*l.* 10*s.*

Italy and her Invaders. By T. HODGKIN, M.A. Vols. I-IV. 3*l.* 8*s.*

Some Account of the Church in the Apostolic Age. By W. W. SHIRLEY, D.D. Second Edition. 3*s.* 6*d.*

Pearson's Exposition of the Creed. Revised and corrected by E. BURTON, D.D. Sixth Edition. 10*s.* 6*d.*

Hooker's Works: the text as arranged by JOHN KEBLE, M.A. In 2 vols. 11*s.*

Bacon's Novum Organum. Edited by T. FOWLER, M.A. 14*s.*

Smith's Wealth of Nations. New Edition with Notes by J. E. THOROLD ROGERS, M.A. In 2 vols. 21*s.*

A Course of Lectures on Art. By J. RUSKIN, M.A. 6*s.*

Aspects of Poetry. By J. C. SHAIRP, M.A. 10*s.* 6*d.*

Geology of Oxford and the Valley of the Thames. By JOHN PHILLIPS, M.A., F.R.S. 1*l.* 1*s.*

A Handbook of Descriptive Astronomy. By G. F. CHAMBERS, F.R.A.S. *Third Edition.* 1*l*. 8*s*.

A Cycle of Celestial Objects. By Admiral W. H. SMYTH, R.N. Revised, etc. by G. F. CHAMBERS, F.R.A.S. 12*s*.

British Barrows: a Record of the Examination of Sepulchral Mounds in various Parts of England. By W. GREENWELL, M.A., F.S.A. With Appendix, &c. by G. ROLLESTON, M.D., F.R.S. 25*s*.

A Treatise on Rivers and Canals. By L. F. VERNON-HARCOURT, M.A. 2 vols. 21*s*.

Harbours and Docks. By L. F. VERNON-HARCOURT, M.A. 2 vols. 25*s*.

Fragments and Specimens of Early Latin. By J. WORDSWORTH, M.A. 18*s*.

The Roman Poets of the Republic. By W. Y. SELLAR, M.A. 14*s*.

The Roman Poets of the Augustan Age. Virgil. By W. Y. SELLAR, M.A. 9*s*.

Lectures and Essays on Subjects connected with Latin Literature and Scholarship. By H. NETTLESHIP, M.A. 7*s*. 6*d*.

Catullus, a Commentary on. By ROBINSON ELLIS, M.A. 16*s*.

Selections from the less known Latin Poets. By NORTH PINDER, M.A. 15*s*.

A Grammar of the Homeric Dialect. By D. B. MONRO, M.A. 10*s*. 6*d*.

A Manual of Greek Historical Inscriptions. By E. L. HICKS, M.A. 10*s*. 6*d*.

Plato: The Dialogues. Translated into English, with an Analysis and Introduction, by B. JOWETT, M.A. 3*l*. 10*s*.

Thucydides. Translated into English, with Introduction, Marginal Analysis, Notes, and Indices, by B. JOWETT, M.A. 1*l*. 12*s*.

A New English Dictionary on Historical Principles. Founded mainly on the materials collected by the Philological Society. Edited by JAMES A. H. MURRAY, LL.D. Part I. A—ANT, 12*s*. 6*d*. Part II. *immediately.*

London: HENRY FROWDE,

OXFORD UNIVERSITY PRESS WAREHOUSE, AMEN CORNER.

Edinburgh: 6, QUEEN STREET.

Oxford: CLARENDON PRESS DEPOSITORY,
116, HIGH STREET.

www.ingramcontent.com/pod-product-compliance
Lightning Source LLC
Chambersburg PA
CBHW020244170426
43202CB00008B/222